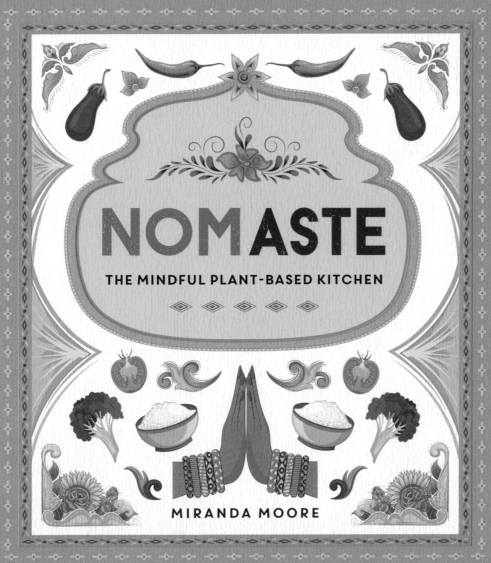

NOMASTE

THE MINDFUL PLANT-BASED KITCHEN

MIRANDA MOORE

summersdale

NOMASTE

An Hachette UK Company
www.hachette.co.uk

Summersdale Publishers Ltd
Part of Octopus Publishing Group Limited
Carmelite House
50 Victoria Embankment
LONDON
EC4Y 0DZ
UK

www.summersdale.com

Printed and bound in the Czech Republic

ISBN: 978-1-78783-819-2

Substantial discounts on bulk quantities of Summersdale books are available to corporations, professional associations and other organizations. For details contact general enquiries: telephone: +44 (0) 1243 771107 or email: enquiries@summersdale.com.

CONTENTS

INTRODUCTION

We are all familiar with the adage "You are what you eat" and it's true: the food we consume really does shape our physical and mental development. But even if we're full of good intentions to transform ourselves into super-healthy, super-grounded gods and goddesses, sometimes it's difficult to know where to start. This book shows you how to bring the ethos and spirit of mindfulness into your daily diet and introduces you to some delicious, nutritious recipe ideas along the way.

Yoga and Ayurvedic principles are based on holistic living, vitality and compassion. If we really want to embrace a healthy, fulfilled lifestyle, it's time to take a look inside ourselves, at how and what we eat and our whole mental approach to food, as well as our psychological well-being and exercise habits. Essential nutrients feed every cell in our bodies and our organs rely on the vitamins, minerals and enzymes we consume to sustain our life processes. This food energy circulates our bodies 24 hours a day as we digest and utilize the elements we need for all of our vital functions.

From learning how to eat mindfully to how to sprout your own macrobiotic foods, turn out your own perfect flatbreads and incorporate a few yoga postures into your day, this book is packed with plant-based recipes, tips and suggestions to help you on your way to becoming a healthier, happier you. It's simply a matter of connecting with our food to improve our health and rebalance our lives, together with embracing the intrinsic joy, energy and self-esteem found in that greater connection. *Nomaste* to that!

CHAPTER ONE:
The Yogic Kitchen

QUIET THE MIND, AND THE SOUL WILL SPEAK.

Ma Jaya Sati Bhagavati

Bringing mindful principles into your kitchen is a natural way to live a more engaged and healthful life. Food is nourishment, and the whole act of eating – of feeding our bodies and minds, and of observing and valuing every item we consume – is a naturally mindful activity. It is no accident that ancient cultures have built entire traditions around food. Even in Western cultures, Thanksgiving and harvest festivals are centred around appreciation for the annual crop. At their roots, these celebrations are about respect and gratitude for nutritious food – and ultimately, respect for life.

How we eat is equally as important as what we eat. Giving our time and attention to the acts of selecting, preparing, presenting and eating food helps to create a deeper connection with the food that nourishes us, leading to a more profound awareness of food as essential to our well-being, rather than simply seeing it as fuel. This chapter will help you start to bring the principles of mindfulness and gratitude into your kitchen.

GETTING STARTED

Here are a few basic ways you can start to think about food more mindfully:

* Observe each item that you eat.

* Notice its texture, its colour, its smell before you eat it, or as you prepare it. Begin with something simple – a blueberry, perhaps, or a salad.

* Observe your hunger.

* Minimize distractions; give your full focus to the food. If your mind wanders, gently bring it back to the food.

* Notice individual flavours, and the consistency and sensations as you chew.

* Take time to really appreciate each item you are eating. Think mindful tasting rather than mindless munching.

* Think about what it has taken for this piece of food to be on your plate: the toil of the farmer, the energy and nourishment from the sun and the rain, the miles it has travelled and the work you've done to prepare it.

* Be grateful for the vitality this food is giving you.

VEGAN?

Some readers will be vegan; others won't be. The recipes that follow are plant-based options to introduce into your diet if you wish to increase the ratio of vegetable-based meals and snacks you eat, while boosting your connection with and respect for plant foods.

BENEFITS OF MINDFUL EATING

The merits of mindful eating extend far beyond the nutritional value of eating healthy food. A myriad of sensory wonders is waiting to be discovered!

A WORLD OF FLAVOUR AT WHICH TO MARVEL

FEELING OF SATISFACTION INSTEAD OF GUILT FOR OVEREATING

APPRECIATION OF FOOD

IMPROVED SELF-ESTEEM

WEIGHT CONTROL

GREATER CONNECTION WITH THE EARTH AND UNDERSTANDING OF OUR PLACE IN THE CYCLE OF LIFE AND LIVING THINGS

FEELING MORE PRESENT, GROUNDED AND CALM

DEVELOPMENT OF A POSITIVE RELATIONSHIP WITH FOOD, CORRESPONDING WITH A POSITIVE SELF-IMAGE

A HEALTHY MINDSET OF GRATITUDE

RESPECT FOR THE EARTH'S CAPACITY TO NURTURE US

NOURISHED BODY, NOURISHED SOUL

Fitness gurus will talk about calories in and calories out. And while it is important to balance the energy we consume with the energy we expend for weight control, this reduces the whole ceremony of eating to an equation.

Instead, yoga gurus propound the virtues of seeing food as sustenance for both body and soul. Eating food that nourishes and energizes your body also nourishes and energizes the mind. Showing respect to our food is also respecting ourselves. Eating mostly plant-based foods, with a spirit of gratitude, demonstrates compassion for the earth and responsibility for our own lives. This ties in with the yoga principles of karuna (compassion), maitri (kindness), aparigraha (simplicity), brahmacharia (wisdom), tapas (self-discipline), santosha (contentment) and ahimsa (non-violence), which collectively contribute to dharma (purpose or virtue).

Aparigraha is a core concept that we can apply to our relationship with food, for it embraces the notion of moderation in what and how much we consume, while cleansing our bodies from the inside. With brahmacharia, the focus is on inner peace and enlightenment, living a spiritual rather than materialistic life. Ahimsa embodies the idea of being gentle and not killing other beings; santosha involves being satisfied with what we have, rather than striving for more; and tapas requires a clear life plan and way of practising, leading to a disciplined life.

PORTION SIZES

With the world population increasing, it's more important than ever that we demonstrate our consideration and consume only what we need. This approach is not only kinder to our fellow humans, but it also engenders more respect for the earth itself. Eating slower and more mindfully, chewing each mouthful more times to aid digestion, goes hand in hand with a subtle reduction in portion sizes and quantity consumed. Eating fast means we eat beyond our appetites, as the brain signal that alerts us that we're no longer hungry takes up to 20 minutes – and in that time we have probably already eaten too much. Smaller portions of nourishing food can help avoid overindulgence and be gentler on our bodies and the world around us.

ARE YOU REALLY HUNGRY?

It can be easy to mistake feelings of anxiety, stress or boredom for hunger. Many of us graze out of habit, or binge when feeling stressed or self-critical. With mindful eating, we can learn to differentiate between genuine hunger and unhelpful cravings.

Overeating is a big issue in our world, and eating with awareness helps us to reset our internal indicator that tells us we're hungry or we've had enough. Similarly, we can avoid or address undereating by eating mindfully since this way of life increases respect for and understanding of our relationship with food.

One piece of wisdom we would all do well to heed is the Japanese ethos of hara hachi bu, of eating until we are 80 per cent full. Hara hachi bu originated in Okinawa, whose citizens have relatively long life expectancies and low rates of heart disease, cancer and stroke.

If you find yourself reaching for a snack, or going back for seconds, take a few moments to consider first whether you really are hungry. It can be a good idea to drink a glass of water, or take a short stroll in the fresh air first. You may find that "hunger" miraculously disappears.

ICED TEA

As soon as spring arrives, I look forward to a daily ritual of iced tea. The tang of lemon and the freshness of mint combined with the coolness of the tea is revitalizing. *Makes: 2 litres*

DID YOU KNOW?

Matcha, green and black teas are all packed full of polyphenol antioxidants – micronutrients that can help aid digestion, help with weight management and ward off diseases.

Ingredients

- 2 tsp black tea
- 2 litres freshly boiled water
- Honey or agave nectar to taste
- Juice and (optional) zest of ½ lemon, plus lemon slices to serve
- Fresh mint leaves
- Ice cubes

Method

In a heatproof jug, make your favourite black tea by infusing the tea in the freshly boiled water until it's brewed to your preferred strength. Add honey or agave nectar and stir in to the tea until it's dissolved, if you like it sweetened. Once cooled, chill overnight.

Remove chilled tea from fridge. Add freshly grated zest and freshly squeezed lemon juice and stir. Serve with lemon slices, fresh mint and ice cubes.

ICED MINT, MATCHA AND LIME INFUSION

As above, but with two generous handfuls or 60 g fresh peppermint leaves instead of black tea, and 1 tsp matcha, served with fresh mint and lime wedges, or mint leaf ice cubes (see page 14) that unfurl with a flourish in your glass as the ice melts. Refreshing and super healthy!

ICED GREEN/JASMINE TEA WITH LEMON BALM

As above, served with lemon balm – a sweet-scented member of the mint family, traditionally used to enhance your mood and increase cognitive function – to cleanse and give clarity throughout the day.

ICED HERBAL TEA

If you don't have fresh ingredients to hand you can always brew your favourite herbal tea from shop-bought bags or loose-leaf blends and chill for an iced version. You could be creative by experimenting with different garnishes.

HERBAL ICE CUBES

What could be more mindful than watching beautiful ice cubes melt and swirl to release the flavour and aroma of fresh herbs?

Makes: 1 ice-cube tray of cubes

Ingredients

- Fresh herbs, such as mint, lemon balm, lemon mint or basil
- Water

Method

Arrange leaves in ice-cube tray. Fill with water and freeze. These herbs work well in both sweet and savoury drinks. You can experiment to discover your personal preferences.

BERRY ICE CUBES

Try berries or fresh fruit, such as raspberries, blueberries, blackberries or redcurrants, or mini slices or zest of lemon, orange, lime or kiwi. Or combinations, such as lemon and mint. These can lift a simple glass of water or juice into something fragrant and beautiful, or add them to your iced tea for added complexity of flavour.

FLORAL ICE CUBES

Edible petals, such as nasturtium or rose work well, or you could try heads of camomile, cornflower, elderflower, dandelion, rosebay willowherb or clover. Prettiness in a glass! Or pop a floral ice cube on top of freshly served soup for a surprise contrast of hot and cold and marvel as it melts. Wild garlic flowers are perfect for this.

TIP

When grating zest, rotate the fruit with each downward stroke to avoid grating the bitter white pith.

A STRESS-FREE KITCHEN

Uncluttered space is a stress-free, happier space, and nowhere is this truer than in the kitchen. As the place where we prepare food, congregate and spend much of our time, the kitchen – or the spot in your home where you eat, if it's not at a kitchen table – is the central core of our home and is therefore a special place. Making it a calming place where you can feel relaxed and joyful will create the ideal conditions for mindful eating. Clear out anything that doesn't need to be in the kitchen and take time to consider how you could make it feel like a lovely, positive space where you can enjoy all aspects of your food. If you enjoy cooking but are hindered by your equipment, perhaps you could save up for some decent basic equipment, such as a sharp knife, good-quality chopping boards and utensils. Or perhaps your kitchen just needs to be tidied up and better arranged to make sure cooking is always a pleasure and you know where to find everything. Arrange your food cupboards in the simplest, most intuitive way, with things that you use most frequently the easiest to access. Or maybe you just want to brighten up your kitchen by bringing in some houseplants or a vase of fresh flowers for the dining table.

SHOPPING

If we want to embrace a mindful larder, we need to look at the ingredients we stock our cupboards with. Buying fresh, organic fruit and vegetables from farm shops, greengrocers and delicatessens, and grains, nuts, pulses, beans, herbs and spices from health food stores can be a joyful experience in itself. It is also nice to know we are supporting businesses we respect. On the other hand, for many people, the convenience of a supermarket is hard to beat. Find a balance that works for you and your schedule.

Making your own food, rather than depending on processed foods, can help us live a more natural, mindful life, and it doesn't have to be expensive. Eating vegetables and fruits in season helps us develop a deeper understanding of the earth's capacity to feed us throughout the year, and can make us very mindful about our menu choices. It also means the food has probably travelled a much shorter distance to get to our plates.

Cleanse your house of chemical cleaning products. You don't need them in your life. Biodegradable alternatives such as vinegar, baking soda, soda crystals and castile soap, plus essential oils for natural scent, do just as good a cleaning job without damaging the environment and human health.

BLUE SPIRULINA CHIA DETOX

Is it a drink? Is it a breakfast? Is it a dessert? You can decide for yourself. This super-healthy blue treat is packed with nutrients and looks almost too good to consume. Take your time to really appreciate its wonders. Between them, blue spirulina and chia seeds are bursting with healthy vitamins and minerals. *Makes: 1 glass/pudding*

Ingredients

* 2 fresh figs
* 3 tbsp chia seeds
* ¾ tsp blue spirulina powder
* 450 ml almond or oat milk, chilled
* Fresh fruit to serve

Method

Use a single serving glass or jar for this recipe. Take one of the figs and cut four cross sections, then place the slices of fig vertically against the sides of the glass for decoration. Place the seeds and ½ tsp blue spirulina in a bowl and mix together with a spoon before spooning into the serving vessel, taking care not to dislodge the fig slices. Set aside to stand.

Blend the almond or oat milk, the remaining fig and ¼ tsp blue spirulina until smooth. Pour half the milk blend over the blue spirulina-coated chia seeds and stir until mixed. Chill for 1 hour until set.

Gently pour over the remaining milk blend to the top of the glass. Top with fresh fruit, such as raspberries and redcurrants, and enjoy observing the flavours and textures. You can drink the top half and eat the lower section with a long spoon. Chill if not eating immediately.

VARIATIONS

Use coconut milk (and a little cold water if too thick) instead of the almond or oat milk, and decorate with coconut shavings. You could try other fruits instead of figs if you wish.

ISKIATE, OR CHIA FRESCA

Iskiate is a traditional Mexican drink consumed by distance runners to boost energy.

Makes: 1 glass

Ingredients

- 450 ml cold water
- 2 tbsp chia seeds
- Juice of 1 lime
- 2 tsp agave nectar or honey
  – honey is traditionally used

Method

Place the water in a glass. Stir the seeds into the water, add in the lime juice and agave nectar and stir until dissolved. Take time to appreciate how much energy these simple ingredients can give you.

BANANA SUPER-SEED BOOST

A banana-based smoothie that will boost your energy any time of day.

Makes: 2 glasses/jars of smoothie

Ingredients

- 1 banana
- 600 ml plant-based milk (oat works well)
- 1 tbsp milled flaxseed mix (milled flaxseed mixed with ground nuts)
- 2 tsp chia seeds
- 2 apricots, dried or fresh (optional)

Method

Blend ingredients together until smooth. The banana gives it an almost fluffy consistency. Pour into glasses or jars and serve.

VARIATIONS

If you like coconut, you could add 2 tbsp coconut milk or coconut yoghurt. Alternatively, 2 tbsp almond yoghurt gives a slight marzipan flavour. A handful of blueberries or strawberries would also be a good addition.

OPEN YOUR MIND TO NEW FLAVOURS

We all have preferences when it comes to food, but a world of taste adventure awaits if you are willing to explore beyond your comfort zone from time to time.

With a spirit of exploration, you can choose to adopt an open-minded approach to tasting new foods. You may surprise yourself. For example, you may consider tofu a savoury ingredient. But why not be open to trying it in sweet dishes, such as chocolate mousse? An attitude of mindful curiosity will help you to become more adventurous in your food choices. However, if you repeatedly try something and still don't like it, accept that this particular food isn't to your personal preference, and substitute for something you like instead.

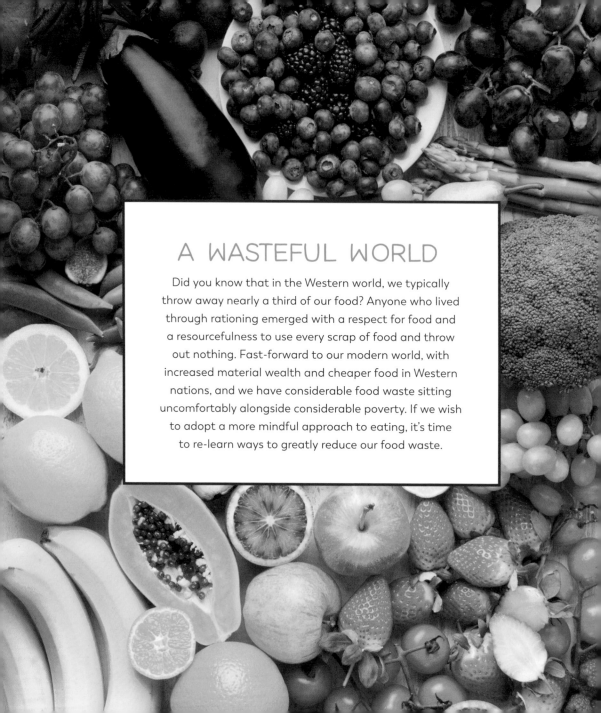

A WASTEFUL WORLD

Did you know that in the Western world, we typically throw away nearly a third of our food? Anyone who lived through rationing emerged with a respect for food and a resourcefulness to use every scrap of food and throw out nothing. Fast-forward to our modern world, with increased material wealth and cheaper food in Western nations, and we have considerable food waste sitting uncomfortably alongside considerable poverty. If we wish to adopt a more mindful approach to eating, it's time to re-learn ways to greatly reduce our food waste.

WASTE-REDUCING CHALLENGE

Get a notepad and draw three columns, headed "week one", "week two" and "week three". Note down every piece of food that you throw out over the next three weeks. See if you can cut right down on your waste by week three.

Week One	*Week Two*	*Week Three*
_____	_____	_____
_____	_____	_____
_____	_____	_____
_____	_____	_____
_____	_____	_____
_____	_____	_____

KITCHEN AND WASTE-SAVING TIPS

Make a note of your food waste. Are there any items that you consistently throw out? If so, adjust your buying habits and buy less next time. (Shopping at refilleries/zero-waste shops or greengrocers often means you can buy in smaller quantities, rather than being forced to buy pre-packaged amounts of an item.)

Consider your shopping habits. Do you do daily mini shops with specific meals in mind, or a fortnightly supermarket shop? Is your way of shopping working for you?

Don't be drawn into two-for-one offers on food that will just go off and end up being thrown out, unless you will definitely use the items.

Store apples, pears, carrots, celery and beetroot in the fridge to keep them fresh for longer.

Plan a weekly menu and buy the required items accordingly. Notice if this results in less waste.

Use tired fruit in crumbles, pies, smoothies, juices, chutneys and jams. Berries that aren't going to be eaten can be frozen.

If you buy a loaf of bread, freeze half of it straight away (pre-sliced, if you prefer) and take it out a couple of days later.

For fresh herbs and chillies, consider growing your own in jars on your windowsill (see page 173). It will deepen your appreciation for them and provide super-fresh ingredients for your meals.

For fruit and vegetables, buying them in smaller amounts, fresh, at least once a week will result in tastier, more nutrient-rich food.

We all have our staples that we always like to have on hand. Keep a "master" list of these so you always remember to stock up on them.

Store potatoes, onions and garlic in a cool, dark cupboard. If any of them sprout, you can plant them in a container of compost and grow some more (see Chapter 7).

Line the bottom of your fridge's vegetable drawer with a couple of pieces of kitchen towel or scrap paper. This will soak up any moisture, keeping your veg and salad at their best.

Use reusable food containers to make your own salads to bring to work instead of buying them in tubs – you are cutting down on plastic waste and using up items that might otherwise be thrown out.

If you don't have a particular ingredient for a recipe, substitute something similar rather than shopping for more food when your kitchen is fully stocked. You will quickly learn which substitutions work and which don't.

When putting away your groceries, don't just place all the new fruit and veg on top of the old in your fridge's vegetable drawer – remove older items and plan to use them the same day. Place your new veg behind your older veg so you can see both and use the older bits first.

Be creative with your leftovers. Use them in soups, stews and stir fries or search online for "leftover [whatever ingredients you have to hand] recipes".

Don't throw out stale bread (but do throw out mouldy bread – mouldy bread should never be eaten). Instead, blitz it in the blender and freeze – it makes a lovely breadcrumb topping for oven bakes. Alternatively, cut into cubes and fry with olive oil, salt and herbs for tasty croutons.

Leave old apples, chopped in two, out on a bird table or dish for garden birds. Apple cores and watermelon skins, flesh side up, will also be gratefully pecked.

For a quick cheat version, simply heat your favourite milk with 1 tsp ground turmeric and a small pinch of cinnamon, stir and enjoy. I like to drink it in an Irish coffee glass.

GOLDEN CHAI

Earthy turmeric, cinnamon and ginger lend this warming drink a wonderful flavour and colour. Simply bliss!

Makes: 1 mug or glass, with extra to top up

Ingredients

- 250 ml plant-based milk (I recommend oat milk)
- 1 tsp ground turmeric, or 2 cm fresh turmeric root, grated
- ¼ tsp ground cinnamon or 1 cinnamon stick
- ¼ tsp ground ginger or 1 cm fresh ginger, grated
- 2 cloves
- Optional: 1 tsp loose leaf black tea (or 1 teabag) – you get a different sort of chai if you leave out the tea
- Optional: a couple of drops of vanilla extract or a few vanilla seeds from a vanilla pod
- 1 tsp raw cane caster sugar, agave nectar or honey

Method

Place all the ingredients except the tea in a saucepan and simmer gently for 5 minutes.

Remove from hob and add the tea. Allow to steep for 3–5 minutes.

Pour through a tea strainer or small sieve and serve. If you used a cinnamon stick, pop it into your mug or glass.

A common ingredient in many Asian cuisines, the finger-sized tuber turmeric gives a vivid golden colour to food and is being studied for its possible use in the prevention and treatment of Alzheimer's disease, due to its anti-inflammatory component, curcumin. Protect your work surfaces when preparing turmeric as it can stain.

YOGA BREAK

Yoga goes hand in hand with mindfulness, and can help promote physical energy, mental clarity and emotional contentment. Here is a posture to help you focus your awareness on your digestion.

CAT, MARJARYASANA – COW, BITILASANA

Cat pose (Marjaryasana) is often paired with Cow pose (Bitilasana) for a gentle sequence. This is ideal for focusing your awareness on your tummy. When flowing from one into the other, the poses help to gently stretch and release any tension in the abdomen and back. With our work and lifestyles, many of us have a tendency to hunch forward for much of the day. Cat – Cow helps to counteract that, gently stretching the abdomen, in turn allowing our digestive organs to operate optimally. Trainer and author Joe Yoon believes Cat – Cow is superior to all other asanas for overall mobility and unwinding, working the vertebrae, chest, shoulders and pelvis. You can perform this before you eat, or any time you have a few minutes to spare.

- Kneel on all fours, with your arms gently straightened and the insides of the elbows facing each other. Start with your back in a neutral table-top position and gently engage your core.

- Leading from the tummy, draw your belly button toward your spine, arch your back toward the ceiling and allow your head to drop. This is Cat pose.

- Still leading from the belly, now dip your spine and gently extend your neck forward and up into Cow pose.

- Slowly move between the two poses, breathing in sequence in a way that feels natural to you. Allow your head to follow at the end of the movement, rather than lead.

- If you like, you can add in a side-to-side motion, going in hoops or figures of eight, in a free movement that feels natural for you. This helps to really loosen everything up inside and release tension you may be unaware of holding.

THE ORGANIC QUESTION

"Organic" has become a term tainted with misunderstanding. Organic food is seen by many as an elitist luxury. However, our ancestors ate an organic diet from the dawn of human existence, until modern pesticides swept into food production. Even the poorest crofters ate a wholly organic diet.

Organic food is food that has been grown naturally, without the use of artificial fertilizers and pesticides and, in the case of livestock, without the routine use of antibiotics. Non-organic farming uses pesticides which pollute soil and water and make their way into our food chain, damaging the environment, biodiversity, human and animal health. According to the Soil Association, food tests have found multiple pesticide residues on many non-organically grown foods. Fruits, crop-sprayed with chemical compounds, are some of the worst affected. The best way to minimize our exposure to pesticides is to buy organic where possible. Eating organic food is a natural extension of the principles of yoga and Ayurveda, respecting purity, simplicity, freshness and non-violence. It's not always available or affordable to each of us, but it's worth taking a good look at what we are putting into our bodies where we can.

£ $ € ¥

It's true: organic food is more expensive. But compare a fresh, juicy organic tomato with a watery tasteless one and there's no comparison in either taste or nutrients. We in fact spend less today on food than at any other time in human history, as expenditure relative to income. Food is cheaper than ever before, because intensive non-organic agriculture has enabled farmers to produce greater yields. We think food is expensive, but that's because we put it lower down our list of priorities than, say, holidays, clothes or gadgets.

Think about how much of a priority you'd like to place on your food and your health, compared with other things in your life. If you conclude that your health is essential, then prioritize by introducing some quality, natural, organic food items instead of processed, intensively farmed foods. You will have to balance this with affordability.

You could begin by converting to just a few organic items, if increasing your weekly food bill is too daunting or simply not affordable. Some of the best items to pick are carrots, apples, potatoes, grapes, berries and soft fruits, since buying organic means you won't have to peel them and are therefore benefiting from their full nutritional value, while simultaneously reducing waste. Organic carrots and potatoes in particular are relatively affordable. A second step might be organic oats, rice and your favourite milk substitute.

MINDFUL TIP

Think about what foods make you feel good and what foods don't. We're often tempted by unhealthy snacks, but end up feeling worse after we've eaten them. Make a conscious decision to buy more of the foods that give you energy and vitality, and cut those that make you feel worse out of your weekly shop. If it's not in the cupboard, you're not going to reach for it! You'll find something nurturing instead. With repetition, this becomes habit – you will begin to automatically opt for healthy snacks as you realize how much better they make you feel.

Start a food journal, with two columns as shown. Note down foods that make you feel good in the first column, and any that make you feel depleted in the second. Stock up on the first list, and eliminate the second.

HELLO! (FOODS TO KEEP)   *GOODBYE! (FOODS TO CUT)*

_____   _____

_____   _____

_____   _____

_____   _____

_____   _____

CHAPTER TWO:
Good Morning!

EATING IS NOT ONLY NOURISHING
FOR THE BODY, BUT ALSO FOR THE MIND.

Thich Nhất Hạnh

The maxim that we should breakfast like a king, lunch like a prince and dine like a pauper isn't just an old wives' tale; it's backed up by science. A study of 50,000 people by Loma Linda University School of Public Health in California found that people who made breakfast their largest meal of the day had a lower body mass index (BMI) than those who waited until dinner, even when they totalled the same number of calories. We burn far more calories during the day when we're active, and fewer during sleep, so these findings stand to reason.

You may not wish to make breakfast your main meal of the day, but a healthy breakfast of fresh, simple food is nevertheless essential to inject energy into your system in the morning and keep you going so you're not flagging by mid-morning. Adequate energy consumed in the morning helps to reduce hunger cravings and so lowers your likelihood of reaching for an unhealthy snack by 11 a.m. A nutritious breakfast really does set you up for the day ahead.

Allow plenty of time for breakfast so you can appreciate its nurturing benefits, rather than rushing and causing stress to your body and mind first thing in the morning.

Here are a few recipes and exercises to start your day in a calm and positive way.

BODY SCAN

This simple but effective meditation will help you to settle into a mindful state.

* Find a comfortable position, lying down or sitting, and focus on your breath, first observing it without judgement, then allowing it to settle, deepen and slow. You can breathe in to a count of four and out to a count of six to encourage deeper breathing, or whatever works for you.
* Perform a mental scan of your body. Starting with your toes, then the soles and tops of your feet, your ankles, calves, shins and knees, shift your focus slowly around your body. Devote a few breaths of focused attention to each body area and observe any sensations you are experiencing.
* Notice if you are gripping anywhere, and gently release – common areas of tension include the shoulders, jaw, tongue, forehead, forearms, buttocks, fingers and toes. Continue to breathe mindfully and release tension on an out-breath.
* If you find your mind wandering, gently let any thoughts come and go without giving them your attention.
* Allow your breathing to return to normal and continue with your day.

TIP

If you find any aches and pains during your body scan, you can return later and focus some attention and intentional breathing on that specific area. Use whatever technique works for you. Some people picture a soft blue spot gently moving around their body and settling in areas that need its calming effect. Others like to visualize an energy field concentrated on a specific site. Or imagine a tight coil unwinding, or a soluble disc placed in the centre of the ache, to dissolve tension. Don't berate yourself if this doesn't work; it can take time and patience to learn to relax and ease tension. Even the most grounded yogis can get tension from time to time.

QUIET SPOT

Think of this as a reboot for your mind. Just as when your computer is slowing up, with too many tabs open, and you need to restart it in order for it to function optimally, a 10-minute daily quiet spot exercise is astonishingly effective at resetting your mind and refreshing your inner interface so everything can operate smoothly. And it's hardly surprising, given that each of us has billions of neurons firing messages around our brains at any given moment. I call it an exercise, but really it's a stilling of the mind and a brief pause in the day to appreciate the world around us through our senses. It's closing down those non-essential apps (any thoughts or anxieties), opening our awareness, and bringing everything back to a clean starting point, clearing the way for mental clarity. With so much noise in the world – both actual and metaphorical noise – a little bit of quiet can be a wonderful thing. My favourite way to start the day!

- Find a peaceful spot in nature if possible, or ideally outside.
- Sit, lie or stand, in a relaxed, comfortable position.
- Note how you feel.
- Allow your mind to still and your breath to deepen.
- Let go of any thoughts that appear, without judgement or analysis – just let them drift away, like clouds in a gentle breeze.
- Observe through your senses – what you see, hear, smell, feel, taste.
- Gently foster an attitude of openness and receptiveness, to really experience the world with its myriad marvels.

- Focus on one or two elements if you like (such as a particular sound, sight or smell, a creature or another living thing).
- Close your eyes and notice your other senses intensify, if this suits you.
- Be aware of the ground supporting your weight and the air flowing in and out of your lungs.
- Note how you feel.
- Observe your awareness of time and how grounded you feel.

Alternatively, try this at lunchtime to make you feel calm, grounded and re-energized to take the afternoon's activities in your stride, or after work, to remind yourself of the endless little details for which to be thankful. You can perform this barefoot if you prefer. I like to lie back, observe the world above and feel my whole body supported by the ground.

FUTURE ADULTS

Many Forest School programmes use this exercise to help children feel calm and connected to nature. How wonderful is that? Common comments after this exercise are: "I felt calm," "It felt like an hour," "I became more aware of sounds," and "I noticed things I've never noticed before."

NOURISH YOUR BODY, NOURISH YOUR SOUL

I make a batch of this every week as I find most shop-bought granolas too sweet. Making your own means you can add a higher proportion of goodies – this version has 40 per cent seeds, nuts, fruit and oil. Healthy fats from nuts and seeds and slow-release carbs from oats will keep you going for hours.

Makes: Just over 1 kg

Ingredients

- 600 g jumbo oats
- Pinch salt
- 3 tbsp coconut oil
- 3 tbsp agave nectar or honey
- 200 g nuts, such as hazelnuts, pecans, almonds, brazil nuts
- 150 g mixed seeds, such as flaxseeds, sunflower seeds, pumpkin seeds, whole or milled
- 50 g currants
- Pinch mixed spice/ground cinnamon

Method

Preheat oven to 180°C. Arrange the oats on an oven tray, sprinkle over the salt, drop in teaspoons of the coconut oil and drizzle over the honey or agave nectar. Bake for 6–10 minutes.

Add in all other ingredients and mix through. You can measure or just add in what looks right, substituting your preference of ingredients and proportions. Bake for a further 5–8 minutes until the nuts have browned, the currants have begun to puff up and the oats are beginning to turn golden. If it needs longer, return to the oven for another few minutes. Check regularly, as it can quickly burn at the edges.

Serve with your favourite milk or yoghurt substitute and fresh fruit.

FOR CHOCOLATE GRANOLA

Add 2 tbsp cocoa powder and 50 g dark chocolate chips.

VARIATIONS

Substitute any favourite fruits and nuts, such as dried apricots, figs or coconut flakes.

GRANOLA

DID YOU KNOW?

An ideal breakfast includes healthy fats (see page 63), a complex carbohydrate that is unrefined and unprocessed – which respects the yoga principle of aparigraha (simplicity) – and protein to boost the amino acids in your blood.

ACAI SMOOTHIE BOWL

An ideal breakfast includes healthy fats (see page 63), a complex carbohydrate that is unrefined and unprocessed – which respects the yoga principle of aparigraha (simplicity) – and protein to boost the amino acids in your blood. *Makes: 2 bowls*

Ingredients

- 20 fresh strawberries
- 1 handful of fresh blueberries
- 2 handfuls of fresh raspberries
- 2 tbsp dried acai berries or acai powder
- 2 tbsp ground flaxseeds
- 4 tbsp almond soya yoghurt
- 300 ml apple juice
- Your choice of seeds, coconut flakes, mint, nuts, berries or other fruit, to garnish

Method

Wash, de-stalk and chop the strawberries, wash the blueberries and raspberries.

Put all the ingredients except the garnish into your blender or smoothie maker, and pulse until smooth. The acai berries and flaxseeds will mean this may need longer than your standard smoothie, and you are looking for a thicker consistency than your morning smoothie drink.

Pour the mixture into two bowls. Top with a sprinkling of garnishes of your choice – coconut flakes and pumpkin seeds add a lovely crunch, but whatever fruits, nuts or seeds you have to hand will work too!

BLUEBERRY SMOOTHIE BOWL

For a different shade of pink, omit the strawberries and use extra blueberries to compensate. For a lilac smoothie bowl, omit the strawberries and raspberries and use only blueberries. To make your smoothie extra-cold, use frozen blueberries.

Garnishing ideas include sliced banana, blueberries, dried goji berries, granola, edible nasturtium flowers and seeds.

Notice the subtle marzipan flavour of the almond soya yogurt blending with the flavours of the berries and seeds. Appreciate that you have made this special and very beautiful creation yourself, and how simple it was to make. Savour it with all your senses, and enjoy the nutrients and energy it is giving you.

OVERNIGHT
OATS

Spare jam jars really come into their own with this delicious breakfast. It's super simple to make and keeps for up to four days, so you can make a small batch each time. Perfect for a blast of vitality first thing!

Serves: One

Ingredients

- 100 ml milk (dairy, soya or nut)
- 100 g porridge oats
- 100 ml yoghurt substitute, or natural yoghurt
- 1 tsp chia seeds
- Optional extras: pumpkin seeds, sunflower seeds, a spoonful of nut butter, flaked nuts, granola, maple syrup or honey
- Topping suggestions: banana, berries, coconut flakes or seasonal fruits

Method

Add all the ingredients except the toppings to a clean jam jar (or other glass jar) and mix together.

Close the lid and place in the fridge overnight. You'll find that the chia seeds have absorbed the liquid by the morning.

Add some mashed banana, berries or other toppings before eating. Observe the textures of the oats and seeds. Marvellous!

BELLY BREATHING

Develop a deeper awareness of the rhythmic flow of your breath with this mindful exercise.

- Find a comfortable position lying down and observe your breathing. Notice how deeply you are breathing, whether your chest is rising and falling, and whether your in-breaths are longer than your out-breaths. Observe this as though you are a detached witness.
- Feel the breath blowing in and out of the nostrils.
- Notice it is cool as it flows in, and warm as it flows out.
- Shift your focus to the air flowing through your throat.
- Observe your lungs filling and emptying.
- Now place your hands gently on your belly.
- Allow your belly to gently rise with each in-breath, and soften toward the end of your out-breath.
- Focus on slowing your breathing. In particular, slow your out-breath.
- Close your eyes and allow your breath to deepen. If your mind wanders, gently bring your focus back to the breath.
- Be aware of your whole breathing cycle, from the air outside your body, to your nostrils, down to your softened belly and back out of your body.
- Continue this for a few minutes.
- Allow your breathing to return to normal.

ALTERNATE NOSTRIL
BREATHING

The focus of this breathing exercise is to connect with your breath, and keep it smooth and flowing. Do not perform this if you have a cold or breathing difficulties.

- Sit or lie in a comfortable position, with your left arm by your side.
- Bring your right hand to your nose. Gently rest your thumb on the right of your nose, and your fourth finger on the left of your nose.
- Exhale completely and then use your right thumb to close your right nostril.
- Inhale through your left nostril and then close the left nostril with your fourth finger.
- Open your right nostril by releasing your thumb and exhale through this side.
- Inhale through your right nostril and then close this nostril.
- Open the left nostril and exhale through the left side.
- Inhale through your left nostril and then close the left nostril with your fourth finger.
- Continue as above, for up to 5 minutes.
- Complete the practice by finishing with an exhale on the left side.

FRESH FRUIT SALAD
WITH LEMON SYRUP AND MINT

An invigorating way to kick-start the day. Not all fruit salads are the same! Compile yours with love and care, and you will be rewarded with a sensory treat. The lemon syrup and mint flavours really lift this into the land of the divine. *Serves: Two*

Ingredients

- Your choice of fresh fruit and berries, such as:
  - 200 g raspberries
  - 200 g blueberries
  - 200 g blackberries
- 2 clementines, divided into segments
- 2–3 cherries, stoned and halved, or 1 plum, quartered
- 1 apricot or nectarine, stoned and cut into wedges, or 1 banana, sliced
- 2 figs, quartered
- Fresh mint leaves

For the lemon syrup

- Juice of 1 lemon
- 2 tsp raw cane sugar or agave nectar

Method

Arrange fruit in two bowls, or one large bowl if sharing.

Stir the sugar or agave nectar into the lemon juice, until it is dissolved.

Drizzle lemon syrup over salad and decorate with mint leaves.

VARIATIONS

Pomegranate seeds also look and taste beautiful as a garnish.

Or you could make this with just home-grown fruit and berries in season to minimize the food miles, and garnish with mint or foraged common wood sorrel, which has a wonderful fresh appley, lemony flavour.

PINEAPPLE WITH LIME MINT SYRUP

Simple, fresh, tangy and utterly delectable.

Serves: Four

Ingredients

- 1 pineapple, peeled and cut into 3-cm cubes

For the lime mint syrup

- Zest and juice of ½ lime
- 1 tbsp fresh mint leaves, finely chopped
- 4 tsp raw cane caster sugar

Method

Arrange the pineapple cubes in a wide bowl.

Mix the syrup ingredients together in a small jug until the caster sugar is dissolved.

Pour the syrup over the pineapple and serve.

GRILLED PEACHES
WITH CASHEW CREAM AND MAPLE SYRUP

Grilled peaches are delicious. This quick, easy recipe will give a lift to your morning. *Serves: Two*

Ingredients

- 2 ripe peaches, stoned and halved (or nectarines work equally well)
- 2 tbsp cashew cream (also known as cashew yoghurt), chilled
- 2 tsp maple syrup
- Fresh thyme sprigs to serve

Method

Arrange the peach halves, cut-side down, on a grill tray. Grill for 5 minutes at a medium-high heat.

Turn the peaches so they are now cut-side up. Grill for a further 5 minutes, until they are beginning to brown. Meanwhile, remove cashew yoghurt from fridge.

Arrange two peach halves, cut-side up, on each plate, spoon over the cashew cream so it sits in the indent left by the stone, and drizzle maple syrup over. Place a sprig of thyme on top of each peach half and serve.

VARIATIONS

Experiment with your favourite yoghurt or whipped cream substitute, such as coconut cream, almond milk yoghurt, Greek yoghurt or silken tofu.

TO MAKE YOUR OWN CASHEW CREAM

You can make your own cashew cream very easily, and use it as a cream or yoghurt substitute. Simply blend 150 g raw cashews with 120 ml cold water until smooth. For a really smooth cream, you will get better results if you soak the cashews in water for 15 minutes first. For a thinner cream, add more water. It will still be slightly granular unless you have an extremely powerful food processor – notice this and appreciate its natural texture as you eat it.

For a savoury cream, add a pinch of salt and an optional squeeze of lemon juice (and use like soured cream). For a sweeter cream, you can stir in 1–2 tbsp maple syrup or your favourite sweetener, although it already has a natural, delicate sweetness. For a cashew dip, you can add crushed garlic, herbs or spices, depending on the flavours you prefer. Other nuts can also be puréed in this way.

WAKE-UP
SMOOTHIES

Start your morning with these jewel-like beauties, and you'll be positively radiating all morning. Not only do smoothies give you a couple of your five-a-day, they are completely customizable to your personal preferences. A fantastic morning boost.

Makes: Each variation makes 1 large smoothie

Ingredients

- 250 ml apple juice
- Ice cubes

For mango

- 1 fresh mango

For kiwi-lime

- 2 kiwi fruits
- Juice of ½ lime
- ½ green apple, chopped

For berry-grape

- Handful blueberries
- Handful raspberries
- 10 strawberries
- 10 seedless grapes (black or red)

DID YOU KNOW?

All these fruits provide an excellent double whammy of dietary fibre and vitamins. For extra nutrients, add 1 tbsp milled seeds.

Method

Wash, peel and chop your chosen fruit. Put the ingredients into a blender or smoothie maker and pulse until smooth. Add more ice for a cooler drink, and more juice for a thinner one.

To save time on the preparation, frozen fruit works well in a smoothie. Wash, peel, chop and freeze your fruit ahead of time – just omit the ice cubes when you make your smoothie.

An exotic alternative to milky porridge to give a warm, delicious start to your day.

Serves: Two

Ingredients

- 100 g rolled oats
- 1 tin coconut milk
- Pinch salt
- Water
- Handful of strawberries and 1 apricot, chopped (or any choice of seasonal fruit)
- Mixed seeds
- Maple syrup (optional)

I rarely measure ingredients; many years of cooking mean I automatically know how much is needed, having learned this knowledge through repetition and practice. I find this simpler and quicker. As you become more confident with these recipes, you will gain experience at gauging how much to use.

Method

Empty the rolled oats and coconut milk into a saucepan and add a pinch of salt. Cook on the hob on a medium heat, stirring continuously until gently bubbling. Stir for another minute or two until it thickens, adding a little water until it reaches your preferred consistency.

Pour porridge into bowls. Arrange fruit on top and sprinkle with 1 tsp seeds. Sweeten with a little maple syrup if desired.

SEASONAL TOPPINGS

You can use any fruit in season. Apple or pear add a nice crunch which contrasts with the softness of the porridge. Raspberries and blackberries also go well with porridge, as do grapes and figs.

QUINOA PORRIDGE WITH RASPBERRIES

As above, except use quinoa instead of rolled oats, and raspberries instead of strawberries and apricot.

COCONUT MILK PORRIDGE
WITH STRAWBERRIES, APRICOT AND SEEDS

DID YOU KNOW?

Mushrooms are a good source of zinc, calcium, magnesium, iron, B vitamins and folic acid and support immune function.

BREAKFAST BRUSCHETTA

Bruschetta is normally served as a dinner starter. This breakfast version has mushroom and fresh basil, to boost immune function.

Makes: 2 bruschetta toasts

Ingredients

- 2 slices sourdough bread (see page 149) or choice of bread
- Extra virgin olive oil
- 10 chestnut mushrooms
- Pinch salt
- Handful fresh basil leaves
- Dried oregano or parsley
- Salt and pepper

Method

Toast the bread slices in a toaster or under the grill. Meanwhile, fry the mushrooms in olive oil with a pinch of salt for a few minutes until soft.

Arrange the mushrooms on top of the toast, and drizzle more oil over. Garnish with basil leaves and a sprinkling of oregano or parsley. Season to taste.

VARIATIONS

Grilled vine-ripened tomatoes instead of mushrooms also work well, served in the same way, with oil, herbs and salt and pepper. Or you could try sliced avocado with apple and a slice of lemon – the sweetness and crunch of the apple contrasts well with the smooth oiliness of the avocado. Look for a contrast of textures and flavours if you try a different combination of ingredients.

Sesame seeds, flaxseeds, sunflower seeds, chia seeds or pumpkin seeds sprinkled on top would all add flavour and nutrition.

WATER IS MAGIC

Drinking enough water is essential for our health. If we forget to keep our fluids up, we become dehydrated. This can lead to fatigue and poor concentration as well as thirst.

The adult human body comprises an average 57 to 60 per cent water. The average adult female needs to consume 2.2 litres a day of water; the average adult male needs 3 litres. Water serves multiple functions in the body, including hydrating our bodies and preventing constipation, a common symptom of a Western diet. Drinking plenty of water can also make us feel fuller, making us less likely to overeat. So make sure you keep yourself hydrated throughout the day, and always have your water bottle to hand.

WATER...

- is the primary building block of cells, essential to the life of every cell
- is used by the body to metabolize and transport proteins and carbohydrates
- is the primary component of saliva, used to digest carbohydrates and aid in swallowing
- regulates our internal body temperature through sweating and respiration
- insulates and acts as a shock absorber to protect the brain, spinal cord and organs
- lubricates joints
- flushes waste and toxins from the body through urination
- carries oxygen and nutrients to cells in blood
- dissolves minerals, soluble vitamins and other nutrients, enabling our bodies to absorb them

MINDFUL TIP

Notice the water as you drink, passing through your throat as you swallow and moving down your oesophagus. Notice its temperature (whether it is cold or warm). Be aware of and grateful for the vitality it is giving you.

CHAPTER THREE:
Lunchtime

**WHEN YOU EAT MINDFULLY, YOU SLOW DOWN,
PAY ATTENTION TO THE FOOD YOU'RE EATING,
AND SAVOUR EVERY BITE.**

Susan Albers

Marking the height of the day, lunch is an important meal that is often rushed or overlooked. Grabbing a quick bite to eat on the go at your desk couldn't be less mindful, so choose to set aside an hour for your lunch if you can, and take your time tasting and chewing.

To avoid rushing, you can be organized about this. You can prepare a packed lunch in the morning, or the evening before. Salads and wraps are super portable, or you could enjoy hot soup in a flask. Give yourself time to eat and enjoy the flavours and nourishment.

A walk, yoga sequence or a spot of gardening is also excellent at lunchtime, to move your body and increase your heart rate, especially if you sit for long periods during the day.

ZOOM LENS

Mindfulness is simply choosing to engage with the world. This activity helps you to practise experiencing little things in life with a mindful mindset.

- Imagine you're a camera with a zoom lens. You can zoom in and out on anything you like. Practise zooming in on one of your five senses, and observe, without any evaluation, what is there. Then zoom out and experience all of your senses at once. Now, zoom into a different sense. You can repeat this for all the senses, or just focus on one or two.

- To use your zoom lens for tasting foods, zoom into the individual flavours in a dish – for example, each separate spice in a curry. Can you differentiate distinct flavours? If not, appreciate how they have blended to create this new and unique flavour.

- Practise widening and narrowing your focus. This is an excellent exercise in honing your mental clarity as you develop your mindfulness practice. Use it with a spirit of freedom and exploration.

Remember how carefree you felt as a child – perhaps running through long grasses in bare feet, not caring who may see you, or pausing to study a frog or a feather on a walk, and being hollered at by an adult to hurry up? With a spirit of curiosity in mind, you can tap back into your innate spirit of fun, freedom and playfulness.

Find a place where you can let go of your inhibitions. It doesn't have to be extreme; simply liberating yourself from tight clothes or contact lenses or letting down your hair, or relaxing your exacting standards and accepting you've achieved enough, can feel freeing. Allow yourself to sigh as loudly as you dare. Even if you feel self-conscious or silly, with repetition you can lose some of the inhibitions that may be constraining you. Carry this attitude into your kitchen with you as you broaden your mind to new ingredients and expand your repertoire to embrace new recipes you've never tried before.

HEALTHY FATS

Dietary fat is essential for brain health and energy. It also makes you feel fuller for longer, so you don't end up snacking on unhealthy options. Plant-based fats in the form of nuts, seeds and oils are high in healthy monounsaturated and polyunsaturated fats. Oleic acid, an unsaturated fat found in olive oils, avocados and nuts, helps to curb hunger. During the process of digestion, it converts into a compound that triggers hunger-reducing signals to the brain. Omega-3 also helps to lower triglycerides (a blood fat), reduce body fat and raise healthy HDL cholesterol.

There are of course villains in the fat world. High levels of saturated fat can increase the risk of heart disease, while trans-fats are artificially created to extend the shelf life of processed foods and should be avoided. The good news is that there are no trans-fats in plants.

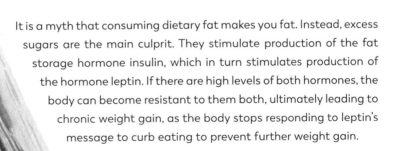

It is a myth that consuming dietary fat makes you fat. Instead, excess sugars are the main culprit. They stimulate production of the fat storage hormone insulin, which in turn stimulates production of the hormone leptin. If there are high levels of both hormones, the body can become resistant to them both, ultimately leading to chronic weight gain, as the body stops responding to leptin's message to curb eating to prevent further weight gain.

SPROUTED LENTIL CAVIAR JAR

Perfect for a light lunch. Make this protein-topped salad in a mason jar and take it with you to work, to the beach, or just out to the garden, park or balcony on a warm day – bliss. *Serves: One*

Ingredients

- ½ small tin, or 110 g, pineapple chunks
- Handful of dark red leaves, such as red oak leaf lettuce, red leaf lettuce, radicchio or pink amaranth
- 6 cherry tomatoes, halved
- 2 carrots, grated
- ½ lemon
- 1 packet sprouted lentils (available from health food stores, or to sprout your own, see page 182)
- Dressing of your choice

DID YOU KNOW?

Lentils are a type of pulse that are high in protein, folate, molybdenum, fibre, tryptophan, manganese, copper, iron, potassium and vitamin B1. Sprouting grains and pulses augments nutrients into more easily digestible forms.

As well as releasing more nutrients, sprouting also releases a different flavour – sprouted lentils taste similar to cress and beansprouts.

Method

In your jar, begin layering with pineapple, then add the leaves, tomatoes and carrot, allowing each ingredient to form a clear layer. Squeeze the lemon over the carrots. Top with sprouted lentils (follow packet instructions if your lentils need pre-cooking) until close to the top of the jar, and add your favourite salad dressing. I like a curried vinaigrette made of 2 parts extra virgin olive oil to 1 part white wine vinegar, with a little crushed garlic, a squeeze of lemon juice and ½ tsp medium curry powder. The acidity balances the flavours nicely, and the pineapple at the bottom is like a surprise mini-dessert to end your lunch. You can take this to work in a sealable jar. If you don't have a mason jar, a used coconut oil jar is ideal – make sure you keep the lid. Expect interested looks from colleagues!

VARIATIONS

Use cooked beans or peas such as cannellini, mung, broad or butter beans or black-eyed peas in place of lentils, and top with a good squeeze of lemon juice and some fresh dill instead of vinaigrette for delicious, fresh flavours and bite.

Capers or chopped gherkin add strong flavour and a different character.

BEETROOT, CARROT, APPLE AND POMEGRANATE SALAD
WITH SESAME AND LIME DRESSING

A colourful, crunchy salad full of fresh flavours and raw goodness.

Serves: Two

Ingredients

- 2 beetroot (raw)
- 2 carrots (raw)
- 1 apple (a crisp, crunchy variety)
- 1 pomegranate
- Mint leaves

For the dressing

- 1 tsp toasted sesame oil
- Juice and zest of 1 lime
- 1 tsp extra virgin olive oil
- Salt and pepper

Method

Using a sharp knife, julienne-cut the beetroot, carrot and apple (cut into matchsticks). Start by cutting off the ends to make the vegetable rectangular. Cut the vegetable into thin strips, about 2 mm wide. Then re-stack the strips, a few at a time, flat-side down, and slice them longitudinally to make sticks. Cut to 6-cm lengths. Arrange on two plates.

Cut the pomegranate in half. Pulling back the hard skin of the pomegranate, gently remove the seeds with your fingers. Sprinkle the pomegranate seeds over the salad.

To make the dressing, mix the oils, zest and lime juice together in a small jug and season with salt and pepper. Drizzle the salad with dressing and garnish with mint leaves.

If you like, serve with rustic oatcakes (see page 158).

VARIATIONS

Add feta (if you eat dairy) or tofu cubes for protein and texture. Feta adds a salty tang that offsets the earthy sweetness of the salad. Chopped fennel or chicory also work well as another crunchy raw and cleansing salad vegetable, each adding another distinctive flavour.

TIP

If you buy organic carrots and apples and young, organic beetroot, and give them a good wash, they won't need to be peeled and you will be benefiting from the abundance of nutrients in their skins. Mature beetroot will probably need to be peeled to remove tough skin.

DID YOU KNOW?

Beans are an excellent source of protein and are high in fibre. Raw garlic has proven antibacterial and antiviral properties (see page 187).

BUTTER BEAN DIP
WITH VEGGIE DIPPERS

A garlicky, protein-rich dip full of flavour and texture.

Serves: Two

Ingredients

- 400 g tin butter beans or cannellini beans, drained
- 2 garlic cloves, crushed
- 2 sun-dried tomatoes or 1 tbsp sun-dried tomato purée
- 3 tbsp extra virgin olive oil
- 1 tsp toasted sesame oil
- Juice of 1 lemon
- 2 tbsp fresh dill
- 1 tbsp fresh thyme
- Salt and pepper
- Sliced chilli, olive oil and thyme to serve

Raw veg for dipping

Assortment of raw vegetables, such as carrot, celery, radish, cucumber, sugar snap peas and chicory, chopped into batons.

Method

In a food processor, blend all the ingredients, adding a little cold water until the desired consistency is reached.

Serve with olive oil drizzled over, and chilli, thyme and extra freshly cracked black pepper.

Dip the raw veg into the dip and enjoy the crunch and combination of flavours and textures.

SERVING SUGGESTION

Serve with flatbread (page 152), pitta, rustic oatcakes (page 158) or crackers. Also good with nachos, tacos or wraps.

For a convenient packed lunch option, simply place in a well-sealed reusable box and pack your raw veg in another.

Try different olive oils and notice the variation in flavour. My favourite is a particular organic extra virgin olive oil, which has hints of lemon and black pepper, but each oil has its own unique character. Extra virgin olive oil contains a higher number of microbe-friendly polyphenols than most other fats.

HUMMUS

A Middle Eastern classic, hummus is a protein-packed powerhouse and cornerstone of vegan cookery. This smooth hummus is slightly spicy, and is fantastic when paired with flatbreads, used as a spread in sandwiches, or as a dip.

Serves: Ten as a dip

Ingredients

- 400 g can chickpeas, drained and rinsed
- 4 cloves garlic, peeled
- 1 tbsp tahini
- Juice of 1 lemon
- Pinch salt
- Pinch chilli powder
- 3 tbsp olive oil
- Olive oil and paprika, to garnish

Method

Simply place the ingredients in your blender and blitz. Add a little water to thin if necessary, and blitz again until smooth. Serve drizzled with olive oil and garnished with any leftover whole chickpeas and a sprinkle of paprika.

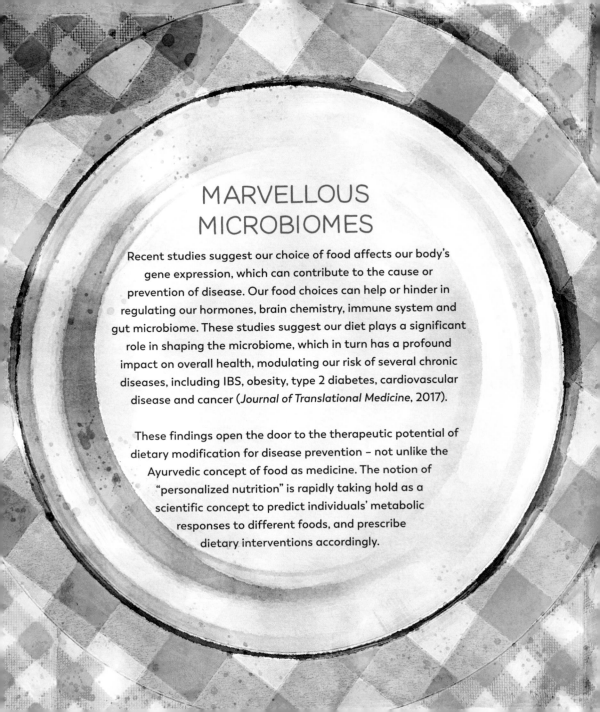

MARVELLOUS MICROBIOMES

Recent studies suggest our choice of food affects our body's gene expression, which can contribute to the cause or prevention of disease. Our food choices can help or hinder in regulating our hormones, brain chemistry, immune system and gut microbiome. These studies suggest our diet plays a significant role in shaping the microbiome, which in turn has a profound impact on overall health, modulating our risk of several chronic diseases, including IBS, obesity, type 2 diabetes, cardiovascular disease and cancer (*Journal of Translational Medicine*, 2017).

These findings open the door to the therapeutic potential of dietary modification for disease prevention – not unlike the Ayurvedic concept of food as medicine. The notion of "personalized nutrition" is rapidly taking hold as a scientific concept to predict individuals' metabolic responses to different foods, and prescribe dietary interventions accordingly.

YOGA BREAK

DEEP SQUAT

Make it part of your daily routine to practise a deep squat before lunchtime, or at midday to harness the height of the day. It does wonders for back health, groundedness and muscle tone, conditioning your back muscles, abs, glutes, quads, calves, hamstrings and pelvic floor. It also helps to stretch the Achilles tendon, which can become chronically shortened with heeled footwear – even with a small heel such as in sports shoes or many men's shoes. Perform your squat barefoot or with thin socks that allow your toes to spread out. You are also protecting your joints from injury by strengthening the muscles around your knees, hips and ankles. Embrace a profound sense of purpose and connection to the earth as you squat.

- Begin in Tadasana, or Mountain pose, with your feet shoulder-width apart or a little wider, pointing slightly outward, and your arms at your side. Then bring the palms of your hands together in front of your chest.

- Keeping your feet flat and evenly spread on the floor or ground, slowly bend your knees, keeping your back straight and your hips level. Make sure your knees track the direction of your feet.

- Using the strength in your thigh muscles, slowly drop your body, bringing your tailbone closer to the ground and increasing the bend in your knees. Continue dropping your body until your heels begin to lift off the floor. Your chest will move forward a little. Pause here for two full breaths, gently pressing your heels toward the floor.

- Slowly rise again, working your thighs and glutes rather than jerking yourself up with a movement of your hips, torso or arms. Keep your hips and pelvis level and allow the strength in your legs and your buttocks to do the work.

- With time, you may be able to squat right down until your buttocks are just off the floor and your hamstrings are resting against your calves, your feet remaining flat and evenly spread on the floor. Allow your pelvis to scoop under a little as you get close to the floor.

- As you increase in flexibility and strength and become more confident at this, you can lower your body to a slow count of ten, hold the squat for five full breaths, then rise to a count of ten. Build this up to a count of 20 down, 2 minutes squatting and 20 up. Feel the strength rooting right down through your feet and into the ground.

COURGETTE LINGUINE
WITH PESTO AND CHERRY TOMATOES

Fresh and delicious for a light bite at home or in a lunch box.

Serves: One

Ingredients

- 1 courgette
- 6–8 cherry tomatoes
- Fresh basil

For the pesto

- 1 small bunch of basil
- 25 g toasted pine nuts (place in a dry shallow pan and cook on a high heat for a few minutes, turning regularly until they brown)
- 75 ml olive oil
- 1 clove garlic, crushed
- Salt and pepper to taste

Method

With a potato peeler, cut long strips of courgette, the length of the vegetable. Then lay these flat in small stacks and slice them into 3 mm strips. Alternatively, prepare the strips using a mandoline.

For the pesto, roughly tear the basil leaves and then put all ingredients in a blender and blitz until smooth.

Arrange the courgette linguine in a bowl. Toss with pesto and cherry tomatoes and serve with fresh basil.

GAZPACHO

MINDFUL REMINDER

Can you single out every flavour? Focus in on each ingredient. Observe how the texture has changed from when you were preparing the vegetables with your hands to the feel of the soup in your mouth, and the sense of replenishment once you have finished.

This beautiful cold Andalusian soup is best made fresh on a hot summer's day. It provides a symphony of flavours, textures and colour.

Serves: Four

Ingredients

- 10 vine tomatoes, cored and diced
- ½ cucumber, peeled and diced
- 1–2 peppers (green if you want to be authentic), diced
- 1 red onion, chopped
- 1–2 cloves garlic, crushed
- 2 tbsp sherry/red wine vinegar

- 75 ml extra virgin olive oil
- Salt and freshly ground black pepper
- 1 tbsp lemon juice
- Handful fresh basil leaves
- Cold water
- Chilli pepper, finely chopped

Method

Chill the vegetables for a few hours before you want to make your gazpacho, if you can. Reserving a handful of raw ingredients for the garnish, place all ingredients except chilli in a blender and blitz. Add a little cold water and blend until it has reached your preferred consistency (I like it smooth but with small chunks for texture).

Serve with fresh basil, diced remaining vegetables, and chopped chilli.

VARIATIONS

Thyme, oregano, rosemary, parsley, chervil, tarragon or chives all work well, or a mixture of fresh herbs. For a contemporary twist, serve it the modern Spanish way: in glasses over ice, with a reusable straw, blended very smooth.

RAW IS QUEEN

Raw vegetables retain all their nutrients so you're getting the full whack of goodness you can possibly get from these glorious, regal ingredients. This vibrant Mediterranean soup is anti-inflammatory and bursting with vitamin C.

BUTTERNUT SQUASH AND LEMONGRASS SOUP

This beautiful creamy soup with exotic Thai flavours can be enjoyed at home or brought to work or to the park in a flask. *Serves: Four*

Ingredients

- 2 tbsp extra virgin olive oil
- 1 onion, chopped
- 1 cm fresh ginger, chopped
- 2 lemongrass stalks
- 2 kaffir lime leaves (optional)
- 1 clove garlic
- Handful fresh coriander, roughly chopped (plus extra for garnish)

- 1 butternut squash, peeled and diced, with the seeds removed
- Zest and juice of 1 lime
- 500 ml water
- 1 tin coconut milk
- Salt and pepper

Method

Heat the olive oil over a medium heat. Add the onion, ginger, lemongrass, kaffir lime leaves, garlic and fresh coriander and gently fry until the onions begin to soften. Add in the butternut squash, lime zest and juice, water and coconut milk, keeping aside a drizzle of coconut milk to serve. Add 2 pinches of salt and some pepper.

Bring to the boil and simmer for 30–40 minutes. Use tongs to remove the lemongrass and kaffir lime leaves then blend with a hand-held blender until smooth. If too thick, add a little freshly boiled water. Serve with fresh coriander and a spiral of coconut milk.

VARIATIONS

For a Thai curry flavour, add 1 tbsp Thai red curry paste (watch out for fish sauce or crustaceans in some shop-bought varieties) before you add the butternut squash.

Use squash, pumpkin or sweet potato in season as available in place of the butternut squash.

ROASTED BUTTERNUT SQUASH SEEDS

In the spirit of zero-waste, wash then roast the seeds with a good sprinkling of salt and a drizzle of flaxseed oil at 180°C for 5 minutes. Delicious! You can also roast pumpkin seeds in this way.

After marvelling at the thickness of the skin as you battled to cut off the tough, protective peel, you are rewarded with the golden flesh!

PSOAS MASSAGE

Self-massage is a powerful tool to help you to devote some attention to your well-being and engage with our powerful sense of touch. The psoas is a band of muscle that connects the front of the lower vertebrae of your spine – just below your ribs – with your thigh bone. This muscle group can become very tight with our modern lifestyles.

Avoid this exercise if you're pregnant. If you have an abdominal health problem, check first with your doctor. If you experience any pain or discomfort, stop the exercise, and try a facial massage instead.

- Lie down on your back and gently bend your knees so your feet are flat on the floor.

- Bring your right hand to your right hip.

- Place your fingertips at the inside edge of your hip, with your elbow facing outward.

- Now press down and slide your fingers diagonally down and to the left toward your pubic bone. You should feel a deep band of muscle. If you can't feel it, try pressing your fingers a little more firmly. If you still can't feel it, bring your right knee toward your chest and you should feel your right psoas engage and contract. Return your foot to the floor.

- Focus your attention on this area and gently massage in small movements, while breathing naturally. You can use your left hand to support your right hand and gently increase the pressure, but never press hard. Gentle palpations are the focus of this exercise.

- For a slightly deeper massage, allow your knees to fall to the left and your right hip to tilt up. The intestines slide away from the area you are going to massage, and you can access your right psoas from another angle. Use your left fingertips for the massage, pointing right toward your right hip, with your right hand supporting. Massage in small movements up to 12 times.

- Return your knees to the middle, with your feet flat on the floor, and relax your arms along your sides with your palms facing up.

- Repeat for the left side.

YOGA BREAK

BODY TWIST

This is great for relieving tension in the back that may have built up during the morning, and for really opening up the abdomen and chest before lunch. Notice if there are any niggly areas, or if one side is tighter than the other. Take a mental snapshot of these areas and return to them later for some focused breathing.

- Lie down and bring your knees up toward your chest.

- Allow your knees to fall to the right and rest on the floor, your left leg stacked on top of your right. Your left shoulder will probably lift off the floor. You can place a yoga brick or cushion under your knees if this is more comfortable for you.

- Place your right hand on the outside of your left knee.

- Stretch your left arm above your head, and then rotate it out to the side, stopping where you feel a strong stretch (you may feel it in your armpit and back).

- Gently twist your tummy round to the left and allow your upper body to follow. Your left shoulder may relax and rest back down on the floor, but don't force this if your shoulder is still lifted. Relax and breathe.

- Allow your left hand to rest on the floor, or in the air if your left shoulder is lifted.

- Gently turn your head to look over your left shoulder.

- Remain in this position for 2 minutes or 20 full breaths.

- Notice your body relaxing and your shoulder easing a little toward or into the floor as your muscles extend.

- To increase the stretch, you can straighten your left leg if you wish, and cradle the outside of your left foot in your right hand.

- Return your knees to the centre, and repeat on the left.

GUACAMOLE AND SALSA

Rich in vitamins, minerals and healthy fat, guacamole and salsa make a killer combo bursting with flavour, and are incredibly versatile. Serve tucked in folded tortilla wraps for a handy and tasty packed lunch, or serve with nachos, tacos or fajitas.

GUACAMOLE

Makes: 1 large bowl

Ingredients

* 3 large ripe avocados
* Juice of 1 lime
* ½–1 jalapeño, or a few slices pickled jalapeños, to taste
* 2 large tomatoes
* Salt and pepper
* Pinch cayenne pepper
* Pinch paprika

Method

Slice the avocados down the middle then twist the two halves to separate. Remove the stone, then chop each half in half again, vertically. The skin should easily peel back from the flesh at this point. Then chop the avocado into a large bowl. Add the lime juice, and mash together until the avocado starts to become a smooth paste – you can leave a little texture. Finely chop the jalapeño and tomatoes, add in and mix well. Season with salt and pepper. Sprinkle with the spices and serve.

SALSA

Makes: 1 large bowl

Ingredients

* 4 vine-ripened tomatoes, chopped into chunks
* 1 red onion, finely chopped, or 2 spring onions, sliced
* 2 tsp white wine or rice vinegar
* 1 chilli, finely chopped
* Juice of ½ lime or lemon
* Salt and pepper
* Fresh basil or parsley

Method

Mix together the tomato, onion, vinegar, chilli and lime juice in a bowl. Season with salt and pepper and garnish with torn herbs. Simple, fresh and delicious.

CORN

When buying tortilla wraps, nachos and tacos, consider opting for corn-based ones, which are higher in phenols than wheat, rice and oats. Phenols are plant chemicals that boost the immune system and combat disease.

SLICED MANGO SALAD ON A BED OF GREEN

Arrange washed young spinach, watercress and rocket in a bowl, top with freshly sliced mango, sesame seeds and optional walnuts or cashews, and serve with sesame and lime dressing (see page 67). This salad is a beautiful fusion of contrasting colours, flavours and textures.

CHAPTER FOUR:
Mindful Snacking

MINDFUL EATING REPLACES SELF-CRITICISM
WITH SELF-NURTURING. IT REPLACES SHAME WITH
RESPECT FOR YOUR OWN INNER WISDOM.

Jan Chozen Bays

Snacks needn't be an unhealthy indulgence. The term "snacking" seems to have evolved to carry negative implications of a shameful activity. Yet our hunter-gatherer ancestors would have snacked any time they foraged for leaves, berries, nuts and seeds. Make and consume healthy plant-based snacks with a spirit of mindful gratitude, and there are only positives.

The following pages contain a few ideas to get you started on delicious snacks that can be prepared and consumed with mindfulness.

HEALTHY MINDSET

Try to let go of any negative associations you may have with food, such as using particular foods for reward, punishment or any other emotional purposes – for example thinking of a dessert or a packet of biscuits or crisps as an incentive for a job well done or healthy food as some kind of penance. This is unhelpful thinking. Think instead of food as sustenance that provides vitality, rather than considering it to be something that can be earned or deserved. In a spirit of mindfulness, you can learn to break any negative associations with food and grow to love food as nourishment and wonder.

FORGIVENESS

Forgive yourself if you stray from your own self-chosen standards. If you have binged or eaten something you were craving that was unhealthy or processed, do not berate yourself. Simply move on, just like in any other mindfulness exercise. Guilt achieves nothing; instead, follow the principle of karuna (compassion) and allow yourself the courtesy of kindness, just as you would encourage a friend not to feel guilty if they had slipped up.

FLOWERING TEA

Flowering tea bulbs are beautiful bundles of dried tea leaves wrapped around a dried flower, to resemble a closed flower bud. Jasmine, lily, chrysanthemum, hibiscus, globe amaranth and osmanthus flowers from Yunnan in China are commonly used, wrapped together with green and white tea leaves. When you infuse them – ideally in a glass teapot or glass mug, to enjoy the full effect – the bundle absorbs water and expands and the flower bud opens and unfurls as you watch, emulating a blooming flower, with the central flower emerging as the centrepiece. They are very hypnotic, and infusing a flowering tea bulb can be a mindful activity in itself. You can buy these at health food shops and online stores. Simply follow the instructions for infusing and enjoy a few moments of tranquillity and the delicate aroma as they bloom.

DIGEST EVERY TINY MIRACLE

CRISPY KALE

DID YOU KNOW?

Kale is an excellent source of vitamins A, C and K. Vitamin A helps with proper functioning of the heart, lungs and kidneys and helps to maintain vision and healthy immune and reproductive systems. Vitamin C also boosts your immune system and is important for the growth and repair of tissues in the body. Vitamin K creates proteins necessary for normal blood clotting, builds stronger bones and protects against osteoporosis.

If you're a fan of crispy seaweed as served in some Chinese restaurants, this super-healthy kale version should float your boat. Every time I make it when friends come over, it rapidly disappears and I'm asked, "How do you make this again?" Kale is a great source of vitamins A, C and K.

Makes: 1 bowl of crispy kale

Ingredients

- 200 g curly or flat kale
  (I find flat works best but either is fine)
- 2 tbsp extra virgin rapeseed oil
- 2 tsp raw cane caster sugar
- 1 tsp salt
- Optional: Chinese five spice and/or sesame seeds

Method

Preheat oven to 150°C. Prepare the kale: if it is a thick-stemmed curly kale variety, cut or peel the leaves away from the chunky stalks and discard the stalks in your compost – the stalks don't roast well and make the dish too bitter. If it is a curly kale variety, cut or tear the leaves into smaller pieces. Arrange the leaves on a roasting tray, making sure they are fairly flat on your tray to avoid getting burnt bits.

Drizzle over oil, then turn the leaves over and move them around to make sure each leaf is coated. Sprinkle over sugar, salt and the optional five spice or sesame seeds.

Roast for 15–20 minutes (check after 15 minutes to make sure it's not burning). They are ready once the leaves have crisped and it is just beginning to brown. A minute or two too long and the whole lot can be burnt.

Shredded spring cabbage can be used instead of kale when in season.

> Cooking at a lower temperature uses less energy, and respects aparigraha (simplicity and non-greediness). If you devote time to food preparation, you can reduce the temperature and extend the cooking time of many dishes, instead of rushing and having to turn up the heat, which uses more energy. Ultimately, this is less wasteful, as you are not using unnecessary energy.

Rich, moist orbs of carbohydrate, fibre and protein, these small but mighty beauties will give you a welcome boost whenever needed.

Makes: 14 balls

Ingredients

- 250 g dates
- 3 tbsp peanut butter
- 2 tbsp cocoa powder
- 1 tbsp ground flaxseeds
- 160 g rolled oats
- 40 g almonds

Method

Mix all ingredients in a blender until they form a thick paste.

Roll into spheres the size of table tennis balls.

You can eat them straight away, but if you can challenge yourself to wait 15 minutes, a quick chill in the fridge will help firm up the mixture. You could mindfully savour one while you wait, or pop a few in a small lunchbox in the fridge to share with friends and enjoy another day.

RAW ENERGY BALLS

RICE PAPER ROLLS
WITH ALFALFA SPROUTS

Perfect paired with a peanut dipping sauce, these light, crispy rolls are fresh, summery and bursting with colour. The alfalfa sprouts add a wonderful crunch, and are highly nutritious.

Makes: 8 wraps

Ingredients

- 1 carrot
- ½ cucumber
- 1 avocado
- 16 large mint leaves
- 8 rice paper wraps
- 1 tub of alfalfa sprouts
- Black sesame seeds

Method

Peel the carrot and chop it into fine matchsticks – a mandolin is ideal for this. Chop the cucumber into matchsticks, and the peeled, de-stoned avocado into thin strips. Wash the mint.

Soak the rice paper wraps in cold water for 1–2 minutes, or according to the packet instructions.

One by one, build the wraps. Arrange the vegetables neatly in the centre of the rice paper, with 2 mint leaves (or more, to taste) in each, and the sprouts on top of the other vegetables. Roll up, then sprinkle with sesame seeds and enjoy with your favourite dipping sauce.

CANDIED ROSE PETALS

What could be prettier? I can't really claim these to be healthy, due to the sugar component, but they're certainly beautiful and delicate, in both aesthetics and flavour, and lend themselves wonderfully to mindful contemplation. *Makes: However many petals you pick!*

> ***NOTE:** You didn't know rose petals were edible? They are, but only pick petals from a rose you know has been grown organically, that has not been sprayed with any pesticides and fertilizers, as you really don't want to be consuming these nasties.
>
> In selecting rose petals, be led by your sense of smell, for they taste exactly like they smell. Choose a fragrant rose, and your candied rose petals will taste divine. I have an intoxicating rose that smells, to me, of orange sherbet. Guess what? The petals taste of orange sherbet. Rose scent is thought to have calming qualities that help soothe anxiety. Be gentle as you gather your petals, and appreciate their natural beauty; pick your petals for colour and appeal, and be grateful to the plant for this gift.

Ingredients

- Handful large rose petals*
- 2–3 tbsp aquafaba (the starchy liquid in a tin of chickpeas)
- 3 tbsp raw cane caster sugar

Method

Place the aquafaba in a small bowl and the sugar in another. Using a pastry brush, dip the brush in the aquafaba and paint each petal, one by one, on both sides. Gently holding one petal between thumb and forefinger, dip it into the sugar, coating both sides.

Carefully place each petal to dry on a non-stick surface, such as a baking tray lined with a reusable silicone sheet or greaseproof paper.

DID YOU KNOW?

Aquafaba, or "bean water", is the starchy liquid in a tin of chickpeas, and can be used as an excellent egg white substitute in all sorts of recipes including meringues.

MINDFUL REMINDER

Really observe the flavour and delicacy of the petal on your tongue as you taste one. Study each petal up close and notice its pigment, veining and silky or velvety softness. Enjoy every part of the process from picking, preparation and presentation to tasting.

A scattering of edible rose petals arranged on coloured crêpe paper in a small box tied with string makes the most marvellous, thoughtful gift for a friend. Your character will shine out in this present, for your friend will be able to imagine you picking the petals, then lovingly and mindfully sugaring them.

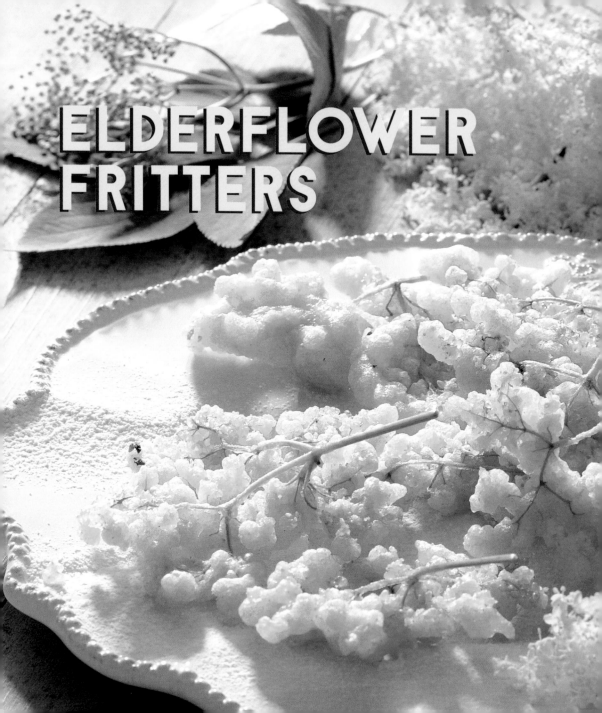

ELDERFLOWER FRITTERS

Beautiful heads of elderflower capture the smell, sight and taste of early summer.

Makes: 4

Ingredients

- 12 elderflower heads
  (freshly picked, preferably in the morning,
  and bug-free)
- 4 tbsp coconut oil
- Icing or caster sugar for dusting

For the batter

- 4 tbsp plain flour
- Pinch salt
- 2 tbsp coconut oil, melted
- 300 ml water

Method

Sift the flour into a bowl with the salt and the melted coconut oil. Slowly pour in the water, stirring until you have a smooth batter. Dip each elderflower head into the batter, holding it by the stalk. Heat your 4 tbsp coconut oil in a frying pan until medium-hot. Fry a couple of elderflower heads at a time in the oil (or however many fit comfortably in your pan without touching), gently nudging and pressing with the back of a wooden spoon to ensure even cooking. Once they have crisped a little (this will only take 2 minutes), remove them and place them on a plate with a sheet of kitchen roll to soak up the excess oil. Put the icing sugar on a flat plate and dip each elderflower fritter into the icing sugar before serving. These are wonderful with a dollop of yoghurt, frozen yoghurt, cashew cream or ice cream.

YOGA BREAK
FLOWER OPENING

This is my own name for this graceful, liberating move, which looks in my mind's eye like a flower bud opening. I find it wonderful for stretching out the back, chest and abdomen.

- Begin seated, with your left leg extended and your right knee bent out to the right, your right foot resting against the inside of your left leg.

- Fold forward over your extended (left) leg with a slight twist in your body so your hands come to the outside of your left leg. As you breathe in, sit up and place your right hand on the floor behind you, with your body supported on your right hand, as you allow your left hip to lift and your left foot to turn inwards until it's flat on the floor.

- Sweep your left arm forward across the front of the body, up and finally overhead as you lift your hips off the floor and open your chest to the sky. Allow this movement to come up through your spine and left shoulder. Stretch your left arm a little behind you as you reach up and back to complete the pose, tilting your head back and lifting your eyes.

- As you exhale, reverse the process and notice when you fold forward over the extended leg how much more movement you have. Be conscious of engaging your abdominal and back muscles to pull your body up and back down, and allow your left wrist to gently flick back at the maximum stretch.

- Repeat slowly five times on one side, then switch sides and repeat on the other side.

If it is difficult to visualize this movement, another way to think of it is to imagine your left hand as the sun rising from your left foot, and sweeping to the right across the sky until it sets behind you, with your arm outstretched and your weight supported on your right arm, and then reversing this on the way back down.

Sesame snaps are delicious, portable, simple to make and packed with nutrients. Perfect for a quick, high-energy snack.

Makes: 20 snaps

Ingredients

* 200 g sesame seeds
* 2 tbsp coconut oil, melted
* Small pinch salt
* 100 g agave nectar or honey

Method

Preheat oven to 180°C.

Place all ingredients in a bowl and mix well.

Spread mixture between two sheets of greaseproof paper (or two silicone baking sheets). Roll out with a rolling pin until ½–1 cm thick.

Carefully peel off the top layer of greaseproof paper and slide the lower sheet (the one with the sesame mixture) on to a baking tray.

Bake in the oven for 8–10 minutes, until turning golden brown on top.

Leave to cool, then cut or snap into sesame snaps. Crumbs can be used as a topping for yoghurt or other breakfasts or added to smoothies.

VARIATIONS

Sunflower seed snaps also work well, or a mix of sesame and sunflower seeds. You could also try pumpkin or flaxseeds, or a mixture of seeds and nuts.

FOR PEANUT BRITTLE

Replace the sesame seeds with salted, halved peanuts.

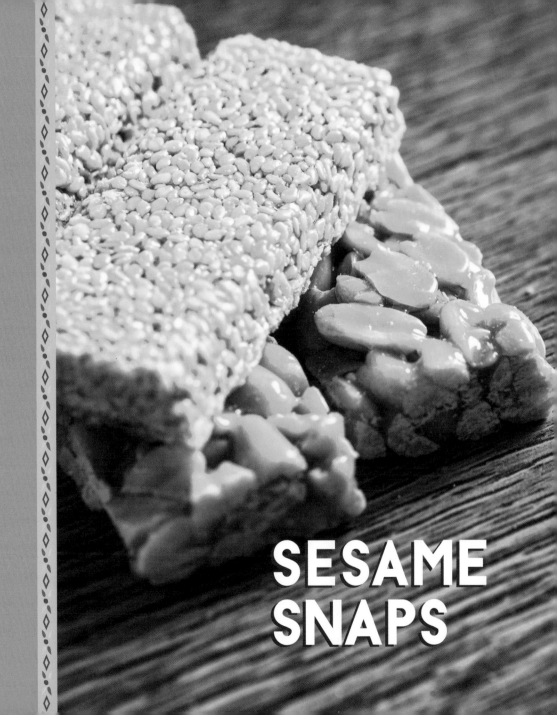

SESAME
SNAPS

PINEAPPLE, COCONUT AND LIME ICE LOLLIES

These beautiful, exotic lollies don't have any added sugar, so they are super healthy – but you can still enjoy the natural sweetness of the pineapple and coconut. They have a thicker, creamier texture than most ice lollies, are fibrous and high in manganese and are relatively calorific.

Makes: 6 (1 lolly tray)

Ingredients

- 400 ml pineapple juice
  (shop-bought or freshly juiced from a pineapple)
- 200 ml coconut milk
- Juice of 1 lime

Method

Mix the ingredients together in a jug. Pour into a lolly tray then add lolly sticks. If you don't have a lolly tray, you can improvise with silicone cupcake cases, small plastic cups or even clean yoghurt pots.

Freeze for 6 hours, checking after 2 hours to make sure the sticks are straight.

FOR MANGO KULFI ICE LOLLIES

These aren't really mango kulfi, an Indian ice cream traditionally made with long-simmered milk, but they're a lot easier and just as refreshing. Increase the amount of coconut milk to 400 ml and blend together with the flesh of one mango, 2 tbsp raw cane caster sugar (or more to taste) and a pinch of ground cardamom until smooth, omitting the pineapple juice and lime. Pour into a lolly tray, add sticks and freeze.

MAITRI (KINDNESS) AND KARUNA (COMPASSION)

Cultivating empathy and compassion, for yourself as well as for others, is intrinsic to a more mindful existence. Plan something kind to do for someone or something you care about. Follow it through. Extend that spirit of kindness, compassion and patience to yourself too. Don't set unrealistic expectations of yourself or others; practise being generous and reasonable. Like any habit, the more you do this, the more automatic it becomes.

MATCHA VOLTAGE CUPCAKES

You're right: these cupcakes thankfully don't have a live voltage. But they're so packed full of energy and so beautiful to behold, they're perfect for a little kick-start at any time of day.

Makes: 12 cupcakes

Ingredients

- 100 g cashews
- 100 g ground almonds
- 100 g dried apricots
- 2–3 tbsp coconut milk

For the icing

- 300 g smooth cashew butter, or home-made cashew cream, see page 51 but use only 60–80 ml water for 200 g cashews
- 2 tbsp matcha powder
- 2 tsp agave nectar

To garnish

- Dusting matcha powder
- 200 g blueberries
- Handful fresh mint leaves

Method

Soak the cashews for 15 minutes.

Blend the cashews, ground almonds, apricots and coconut milk until they form a smooth paste. You will need to scrape down the nuts and lumps from the edges and re-blast to make sure it is fully blended. You may need to do this a couple of times.

Spoon the mixture into a well-oiled cupcake tray, dividing it into 12 cupcakes. If you have silicone cupcake cases, use these to line the tray, or invest in a silicone cupcake tray. Press down with a spoon so the mix is firm.

To make the icing, mix the matcha powder and agave nectar into the cashew cream, either with a blender or in a bowl. You may need to add a little water. Spoon this icing mix over the bases. Chill for 3 hours.

Remove from fridge. Carefully remove each cupcake from the tray. If your tray is made of silicone or you have used silicone cases, this will be straightforward. If not, you will need to gently lever each cupcake out of the tray by placing two dinner knives on either side and pushing slightly for them to come free from the tray. If they are difficult to remove, you may also need to gently twist a knife round the edge to loosen first, taking care not to scratch your tray. It may be slightly fiddly but it will be worth it.

Dust with a little matcha powder and decorate with a trio of blueberries and a couple of mint leaves on top. Admire your handiwork and marvel that you made this beautiful creation from gifts bestowed by nature. Observe all the different textures and flavours blended together as you eat.

VARIATION

For avocado-cashew icing, substitute one avocado, shelled and stoned, for 100 g of the cashew cream. Press through a sieve and mash into the icing, or mix in a blender.

UNNI APPAM
BANANA FRITTERS

Unni Appam is a traditional Keralan snack; think of 'spiced-up' banana fritters and you're close. You'll need a mini ball cake pan for this recipe.

Makes: Approximately 18 balls

Ingredients

- 50 g fresh coconut, finely chopped
- 120 ml jaggery or 120 g muscovado sugar
- 60 ml water
- 115 g rice flour
- 35 g whole wheat flour
- 1 ripe banana
- Pinch sea salt
- Pinch baking powder
- ½ tsp cardamom powder
- 1 tsp roasted sesame seeds
- Oil, for frying

Method

Gently toast the coconut in half a teaspoon of oil until golden; leave to cool. Heat the jaggery in a small pan with water until melted; sieve and leave to cool. Dry toast the flours for about a minute. Mash the banana until smooth.

Mix the coconut, jaggery, banana and flours, adding enough water to create a smooth batter of dropping consistency. Leave for 15 minutes at room temperature, covered with a clean tea towel, and then add the remaining ingredients and mix to combine.

Preheat the oven to 200°C, pop a teaspoon of oil in each hole of the mini ball cake pan and heat for 3–5 minutes.

Add 1 tablespoon of the mixture to each hole and cook until air bubbles form on the surface; flip them over and cook the other side. They're ready when a cocktail stick comes out cleanly with no raw batter.

LEMON BARLEY WATER

This is something we associate with previous generations, but a glass of lemon barley water with ice is a wonderful refresher on a hot, sunny day.

Makes: Just over 2 litres

Ingredients

- 100 g pearl barley, rinsed
- Rind of 1 lemon
- 40 g raw cane caster sugar
- 2 litres water, freshly boiled
- Juice of 2 lemons
- Ice cubes and lemon slices, to serve

Method

Place the barley in a large heatproof jug and add the lemon rind and sugar. Pour over the boiled water, stir to dissolve the sugar and leave to cool. Chill overnight or for at least 6 hours.

Remove from fridge and add the lemon juice. Stir well.

Strain and serve with ice cubes and a slice of lemon. You can use the barley in a soup, stew or salad – they won't need to be cooked.

GREEN QUEEN NECTAR

Whoever said blue and green should never be seen hasn't beheld this beautiful juice. Spinach is high in iron, folate, potassium, beta carotene and B and C vitamins.

Makes: 2 jars or glasses

Ingredients

* 100 g young spinach
* 100 g blueberries
* 500 ml apple juice, chilled
* 1 tsp spirulina powder
* Ice cubes to serve

Method

Blend ingredients together until smooth. If you prefer it thinner, you can juice the spinach before blending, reserving the pulp for use in a soup or sauce, or wilt the spinach in a little hot water or in a steamer first. Pour over ice and enjoy.

YOGA BREAK

UPWARD SALUTE, URDHVA HASTASANA

This standing asana is the first posture of Surya Namaskara (Sun Salutation) sequences and lifts the body to embrace the energy of the sun. Since the sun provides the light and heat that give life to all living things on Earth, it seems like a worthwhile posture to include here.

Traditionally, when performed as part of a Sun Salutation sequence, this asana is performed outside, facing east toward the rising sun. When practising this uplifting, energizing posture, it is helpful to hold the concept of release in mind. Feel powerfully rooted as you perform your salute.

- Begin by standing with your feet hip-width apart and your arms resting by your sides.
- On an in-breath, slowly and with focus sweep your arms out to the sides and very slightly backward, and up and overhead until your palms meet, with your fingers reaching skyward. Your arms should be stretched straight, with your hands active right through the fingertips. At the same time, bring your gaze and your head skyward too, toward your thumbs. Slide your shoulders away from your ears, with your shoulder blades down and flat against your back. Keep your thighs strong and your feet evenly spread, but do not lock the knees, and avoid arching your back – keep your tailbone tucked in and your hips level.
- Exhale and lower your arms back out to the sides and down to release the pose.
- Repeat two more times if you like.

THE SIX TASTES

Ayurveda sees rasa, or taste, as a vital therapeutic tool that is critical in determining the effect various foods will have on our physical, mental and spiritual state.

The six tastes – sweet, sour, salty, pungent, bitter and astringent – combine in countless ways to create the incredible diversity of flavours we encounter in food, and, in Ayurvedic thinking, each one contributes to dietary and psychological balance. Our sense of taste can tell us a great deal, and even the same item can vary enormously in taste depending on different conditions or processes it has undergone.

You don't have to be a follower of Ayurveda to appreciate the value in taking time to really experience the variety of flavours we encounter and be open to their active, therapeutic potential. Be aware of rasa as you eat by cutting out all other distractions and really focusing in on your sense of the taste.

CHAPTER FIVE:
Evening Meals

WHEN YOU BOW, YOU SHOULD JUST BOW;
WHEN YOU SIT, YOU SHOULD JUST SIT;
WHEN YOU EAT, YOU SHOULD JUST EAT.

Shunryu Suzuki

Rituals centred around dinner time can help to frame our main meal of the day as something that is worthy of our attention and care, transforming the act of eating into an intimate ceremony of sharing and respect.

Learn to see meal times as a calm place; an entity in their own right. Set aside adequate time so dinner isn't rushed. Turn off distractions. Clear the table and keep the kitchen uncluttered. Give thanks for your day or share an anecdote or observation. Light a candle, perhaps, or consider soft lighting. Whether or not you are religious, verbally thanking the earth, sun and water for the food on your plate is another possibility to consider. Eat slowly and mindfully, and give every family member respect and space. Just as every seedling needs space and the right conditions to thrive, we do too!

Make this a time of sanctuary – a sacred time in your day and your home – and you will reap the rewards of more engaged, more connected meals, with the physical act of eating becoming an opportunity for a deeper connection with food, nature and the people we dine with. If you live alone, give the care and respect to yourself that you would to a guest.

DINNER RITUALS I CAN PERFORM:

_____

_____

_____

TUNE IN TO YOUR SENSES

In a mindful kitchen, it's as much about appreciating the process as it is about the results. This is a sensory life, and you are a sensory being; in being mindful, we are simply becoming more attuned to our sensory perception. Observe an onion as you chop it; notice the physical sensations and the smell. Be conscious that this food came from the soil, and be grateful for this gift of nourishment. Notice the feel of a fork in your hand or against your lips and tongue. Invest in plain, simple crockery that allows the colours to stand out from your plate.

If you want to take it a step further, you could book yourself on a pottery course and make your own bowl, plate and mug set. This is a wonderful activity to really connect everything together, from the clay in the ground to the cool smoothness of the clay between your hands, the colours of the glaze, the transformation as your creations are fired, and finally sitting down to eat a meal from your own plate.

If you prefer the idea of working with wood, you could buy a whittling book and carve your own spatulas and spoons, then use them for preparing and eating these and other recipes.

RESPECTFUL CONVERSATIONS

Practise really listening. This is one of the greatest life skills we can learn and one of the greatest gifts we can give the people in our lives. If you find yourself wanting to jump into a conversation to give your two cents, practise discipline. Show respect to the speaker and give them your full attention. Once you make this a habit, you will be rewarded with friends who greatly value your genuine care and attention.

VIETNAMESE ALMOND CURRY

Full of fresh vegetables and spices, Vietnamese street food is super healthy and delicious. Serve with brown basmati rice with a handful of wild rice mixed through. The black strands look beautiful and pick up the black of the beans in the curry.

Serves: Five

Ingredients

- 5 spring onions, chopped
- 1 leek, chopped
- 3 cloves garlic, chopped
- 2 cm fresh ginger, cut into small chunks
- 1 green chilli
- 1 lemongrass stalk
- 4 cardamom pods
- 1 pumpkin or butternut squash, peeled and diced into large cubes – keep the seeds for roasting (see page 79)
- 1 courgette, diced
- 1 tin black beans, black-eyed peas or chickpeas – if using chickpeas, reserve the aquafaba (see page 95)
- 2 tins coconut milk, or 1 tin coconut milk and 400 ml water
- 2 tbsp coconut or olive oil
- 6 tbsp almond butter
- 2 tbsp tamari or soy sauce
- 2 tbsp medium curry powder or garam masala, or 3 tsp ground coriander, 2 tsp ground turmeric and 1 tsp ground cumin
- Juice of 2 limes – reserve the zest to make lime zest ice cubes (see page 14)
- Salt and black pepper to taste
- Handful flaked almonds and beansprouts to serve
- Lime wedges

Method

Preheat oven to 160°C. Fry the onion, leek, garlic, ginger, chilli, lemongrass and cardamom in oil for 2 minutes over a low to medium heat. Arrange all the vegetables and the beans in a casserole dish, and add the cooked ones.

In a large jug, mix together all the wet ingredients, including the almond butter, and the spices, and season. Pour over the vegetables, adding a little water if needed.

Roast for 45 minutes–1 hour, to allow the flavours to blend and deepen (you could also cook this in a slow cooker on low). Remove the lemongrass with a spoon, and remove or keep in the cardamom as you choose. Serve with rice, flaked almonds and beansprouts and a wedge of lime.

RATATOUILLE

This hearty vegetable stew is the ultimate comfort food, and is perfect served with crusty sourdough and a leafy green salad. Slow cook it to encourage the flavours to really emerge.

Serves: Four

Ingredients

- 2–3 onions, peeled and roughly chopped into large chunks
- 2 courgettes, chopped into chunks
- 2 peppers (ideally one red, one yellow, but any colour is fine), chopped into chunks
- 1 aubergine, chopped into chunks
- 4–6 cloves garlic
- 4 vine-ripened tomatoes, cored, peeled and chopped, or 1 tin chopped tomatoes
- 1 tbsp tomato purée
- 3 tbsp extra virgin olive oil
- 1 tsp paprika
- 2 tsp thyme
- 1 tsp oregano
- ½ tsp rosemary
- Generous handful fresh basil leaves
- Sea salt and black pepper, to taste
- Fresh herbs to garnish, such as parsley, basil and rosemary
- 1 lemon, quartered

Method

Place all ingredients except for the fresh herbs and lemon in a slow cooker or oven dish. Turn your slow cooker to low, or your oven to 90°C. Cook for 6–8 hours.

Remove from slow cooker or oven, garnish with fresh herbs and serve with lemon quarters to squeeze over. Many recipes will ask you to fry the onion, aubergine, courgette and garlic first, or roast the ratatouille for a much shorter time, but I find this slow-cook version allows all the flavours to really come into their own. It is also gratifyingly simple and satisfying. You can put it on in the morning and it'll be ready when you get home!

VARIATIONS

You could add 8 medium potatoes, halved (no need to remove the skins) to the dish, for a single pot dinner.

Some people thinly slice the vegetables into discs and arrange them in a ring around the edge of their oven dish, which looks spectacular. I personally love the rustic simplicity, look and texture of large chunks, but thin slices melt in the mouth and look great for a fine dining presentation. You and your guests will love it either way.

GREEN SALAD

Arrange lettuce, spinach, rocket and watercress in a salad bowl. Sprinkle a few mixed seeds over, and a few leaves of basil or coriander if you wish.

A handful of beet leaves, with their claret stalks, gives a beautiful touch of contrasting colour and a deep, earthy flavour. Chard, with its vivid yellow, fuchsia and white stems, can add a multicolour quality – hence the term rainbow chard.

A WORLD OF PLANTS

Healthy, plant-based food includes every part
of a plant, above and below ground:

Remember to eat food from each of these plant groups a couple of times every week.

- Leaves include spinach, kale, lettuce, Brussels sprouts and cabbage.

- Stems include celery, asparagus and rhubarb.

- Seeds include sesame/chai/flax/sunflower/pumpkin
  seeds, sweetcorn, peas, beans and pulses.

- Fruits include aubergine, cucumber, tomato, pumpkin and berries.

- Flowers include broccoli, cauliflower and edible flowers.

- Roots include carrot, beetroot, parsnip, radish, turnip and swede.

- Tubers include potato, ginger, yam, turmeric, galangal, cassava and arrowroot.

- Bulbs include garlic, onions, spring onions and leeks.

- Cereals from grains include rice, wheat, corn and barley.

- Oils from fruit/seeds/nuts include sunflower, coconut, olive and nut oils.

Between them, these plant foods contain a profusion of vitamins and minerals, including calcium, potassium, folic acid, magnesium, iron, beta carotene, phosphorus, zinc, sodium and vitamins B3, B5, B6, B12, C, E and K. Each performs an essential function in our health.

ROOTS

Make sure you don't overlook roots. Roots are wonderful foods, literally increasing our connection with the earth. Take that connection further by allowing yourself to feel grounded as you handle, prepare and eat them (and even plant and dig them up too, if you are so inclined).

IMAM BAYILDI

Another stunning roasted veg recipe, this rich Turkish dish is a fusion of fleshy aubergine, garlic, onion and tomato flavours. Serve with Turkish flatbread (see page 152) and salad. Also delicious hot or cold the next day. You could freeze a batch and defrost as required. Imam bayildi translates as "the imam swooned" (after tasting this dish)! *Serves: Four*

Ingredients

- 4 tbsp extra virgin olive oil
- 2 onions, finely chopped
- 4 cloves garlic, crushed
- 1 tin chopped tomatoes
- 1 tsp parsley
- Small pinch cinnamon
- Small grating nutmeg (or ½ tsp dried nutmeg)
- Salt and pepper to taste
- 4 aubergines
- Juice of ½ lemon (optional)
- Fresh mint

Method

Preheat oven to 180°C. Fry the onions in 1 tbsp olive oil until softened. Add the garlic, tomatoes, parsley, cinnamon, nutmeg, salt and pepper. Cook until the mixture thickens.

ROASTED VEG

Roasted vegetables are amazingly versatile. Take whatever seasonal veg you have to hand – cut into chunks, sliced into strips, or diced – and arrange in a roasting dish or oven tray, with a sprinkling of salt and herbs. Alternatively, take care arranging vegetable pieces on kebab skewers. Bake at 180°C for 25–40 minutes, depending on your oven and how browned you like your veg, and they will be delicious served with breads, pasta, potatoes, rice or quinoa, or used as a pizza topping or pie filling. For a quick and easy roasted veg pizza-tart, simply line the base of a greased pie dish or a flat oven tray with a sheet of puff pastry, top with roasted veg and bake at 180°C for 20 minutes. If your pie base is placed on an oven tray, gently push the edges in to create a ridge round the edge.

To prepare the aubergines, cut each in half lengthways, from stem to base. Score the flesh several times lengthways, about 3 cm deep, taking care not to pierce the skin.

In a medium frying pan, fry the aubergines cut-side down in the remaining oil for 2 minutes. You will notice they absorb much of the oil. Turn and fry on the skin-side for two more minutes, then remove from heat.

Scoop out the flesh of each aubergine and mix with the tomato mixture, then spoon the mixture back into each aubergine skin. Squeeze over the lemon juice.

Arrange the stuffed aubergines in an oven dish and bake for 35–40 minutes.

Traditionally, it is chilled, garnished with mint and served cold the next day, with flatbread and a spoon of yoghurt. Or you could eat it hot, with bread, couscous, bulgur wheat, quinoa or buckwheat.

The sweet flavours of the tomatoes and onions in this tart set each other off perfectly, and it's ideal for sharing.

Serves: You decide! (Served with salad, this will serve two as a main, or can stretch to more if served as an appetizer or snack.)

Ingredients

- 6 onions, sliced horizontally into rings
- 3 tbsp extra virgin olive oil
- 2 tbsp maple syrup (or agave nectar)
- 400 g bread dough or puff or filo pastry
- 600 g ripe tomatoes – mix of different varieties and sizes, sliced horizontally
- Optional: fresh herbs, such as thyme, dill or rosemary
- Salt and pepper
- 2 handfuls fresh rocket leaves
- Balsamic vinegar
- 2 handfuls watercress

Method

Preheat oven to 180°C.

Arrange onions in a roasting dish. Mix olive oil together with the syrup. Pour a third of this over the onions. Roast the onions for 20 minutes until caramelizing and sweet-smelling, then remove and turn oven to 190°C.

Roll out dough or pastry into a rectangle, roughly 35 cm x 25 cm. Arrange caramelized onions in a layer, then arrange tomato slices on top. Pour over the remainder of the olive oil and syrup mixture. Add a little thyme or rosemary, if using, and season with salt and pepper.

Bake for 15 minutes. Remove from oven and cut into slices or triangles with a pizza cutter. Decorate with some fresh rocket and fresh dill, if using, and serve with balsamic vinegar and a simple side salad of rocket and watercress.

CARAMELIZED TOMATO AND ONION TART

OTHER TART IDEAS

CARAMELIZED BEETROOT, ONION AND WALNUT FILO TART

Sweet and earthy flavours combine in this pretty-as-a-picture tart. Caramelize slices of beetroot and onion together. Cut a disc of filo pastry, 10 cm in diameter (or larger, if you are using a larger tart tin). Place on a roasting tray or tart tin, top with caramelized beetroot and onion mixture, add a few whole walnuts and pour over oil and syrup mixture. Bake for 25 minutes at 190°C. Serve with a small crumbling of feta or tofu pieces, if you like.

SWEET POTATO AND SPINACH FLAN WITH SILKEN TOFU AND CASHEW CREAM

The sweet potato "pastry" benefits from being flour-free, as well as looking and tasting divine. A sweet potato pie case is super easy – simply thinly slice a sweet potato and arrange it in a greased tart tin, overlapping slices to fill any gaps until the tin is lined with sweet potato. No other ingredients required for the tart case! Bake for 15 minutes at 180°C.

For the filling, mix young spinach with silken tofu and cashew cream. Take the tart case out of the oven, pour in your filling and bake for a further 30–35 minutes at 180°C. Serve with fresh spinach leaves topped with seeds.

FOOD MEDITATION

This is an excellent meditation to deepen your connection with food, and to pause to observe your senses.

- Take a plant-based piece of food that fits in the palm of your hand.

- Focus your attention on the item. How does it feel in your palm? How does it feel between your thumb and finger? Observe the texture. Be aware that you are experiencing it through all of your senses. How does it smell? Examine your food item close up. Do you notice anything about it?

- Have a taste. What flavours do you observe? How do you experience the textures on your tongue? Does it crunch as you bite in? How about the temperature? Notice any sensations.

- Be aware that this piece of sustenance has come from the earth. Consuming it is part of the natural life cycle of both the plant and you.

DIFFERENT STATES MEDITATION

Another food meditation to try, once you have mastered the basic food meditation. The idea is to observe the same item in different states. This really extends your mindfulness practice. You can try this with just about any food.

SOME SUGGESTIONS:

Uncooked dough/bread/toast

Cold water/hot water/ice

Fresh fig/dried fig/fig yoghurt/fig jam/stewed fig (in a pie or crumble, perhaps)

White grape/raisin/balsamic or white wine vinegar/grape juice or white wine

Red grape/currant/red wine vinegar/red grape juice or red wine

Ripe tomato/sundried tomato/grilled tomato/cooked tomato sauce/passata/tomato purée/tomato juice

- Choose an item of food that you like, and get hold of it prepared in different states like the examples above. Place them all in front of you on your kitchen table.

- Observe each version of the same food. Notice how each looks, smells and feels. Be aware of your senses.

- Taste each item in turn, and notice any sensations or impressions.

- Observe how the same original food has changed in state in response to different human interventions (even better if you grew or prepared some or all of the item states yourself – this will deepen your connection with this food in its different states).

- Notice how the addition of processes such as heating or pressing or the addition of other ingredients has altered the food from its original state.

- Marvel at how we can appreciate one item of food in so many different ways, and acknowledge the incredible versatility of these remarkable gifts of nature.

GLASS NOODLES
WITH STIR-FRY VEGETABLES AND SOY SAUCE

Glass or cellophane noodles are starchy noodles made from mung bean, potato, sweet potato or tapioca starch and water. They are also known as bean thread noodles or Chinese vermicelli.

A light and nutritious meal, perfect at the end of summer when the vegetables are in season. It is simple to make and ready in minutes.

Serves: Two

Ingredients

- 1 red pepper, sliced into strips
- 1 yellow pepper, sliced into strips
- 1 green pepper, sliced into strips
- 1 aubergine, sliced into strips
- 1 courgette, sliced into strips
- 1 chilli, finely chopped
- 100 g glass noodles

- 1 tbsp sesame oil
- Soy sauce
- 1 lime, quartered
- Black pepper
- A few leaves of parsley
- Dried chilli flakes

Method

Fry the vegetable strips in the oil for 3 minutes, so they still have a bite to them and aren't too soft. If you have a wok, use this, otherwise you may need to use two frying pans.

Meanwhile, place the noodles in a saucepan and pour over enough boiled water to cover. Simmer for 2 minutes on the hob. (Alternatively, you can place the noodles in a heatproof bowl, pour over boiled water and leave them for 5 minutes.) Drain.

Arrange the noodles between two bowls, top with the vegetables and serve with soy sauce, lime wedges, freshly cracked black pepper and parsley, plus chilli flakes to taste.

MINDFUL TIP

Appreciate that the array of different colours and flavours of this dish were grown with minimal violence, respecting ahimsa.

BEETROOT BURGERS WITH GUAC

Try these beetroot and quinoa burgers for a healthy and delicious twist on a classic – it's far easier and faster than you might think.

Makes: 8 burgers

Ingredients

- 1 medium red onion
- 1 red pepper
- Oil for frying
- 4 cloves of garlic, minced
- 1 large bunch of coriander, chopped
- ½ can black beans, drained and rinsed
- 1 beetroot, finely grated
- 175 g cooked quinoa (made according to the packet instructions)
- 150 g breadcrumbs
- 1 tsp chilli flakes
- 1 tsp chilli powder
- ½ tsp smoked paprika
- 1 tbsp tapioca flour
- Charcoal bun, pitta or other roll
- Salad leaves
- Guacamole

Method

Peel and finely chop the onion. Remove the stem and seeds from the pepper and finely chop. Cook in a little oil for around 8 minutes – until the vegetables become less wet. Add the garlic and chopped coriander and cook for a further 1–2 minutes.

In your food processor, process half the black beans on a medium speed to form a dough. In a large bowl, add the processed and unprocessed beans, beetroot, quinoa, breadcrumbs, cooked vegetables and spices. Mix well so that the ingredients are evenly distributed.

Form the mixture into small patties – it will be sticky and thick at this point. Over a medium heat, preheat a little oil in a frying pan, then fry the patties, turning halfway through. Drain on kitchen paper before serving in a charcoal bun or burger roll of your choice, with salad leaves and plenty of fresh guacamole (see page 82).

SATAY KEBABS
WITH PEANUT AND LIME DIPPING SAUCE

Delectable kebabs with sauce so delicious it will make your eyes and shoulders soften with joy. A feast for all the senses. *Makes: 6 kebabs*

You will need: 6 skewers (if using bamboo skewers, soak them in water for 5 minutes first)

Ingredients

- 1 onion, cut into large chunks
- 9 chestnut mushrooms, halved
- 18 cherry tomatoes
- 1 block of extra-firm tofu, cut into 3-cm cubes
- 1 courgette, cut into large chunks
- 1 green pepper, cut into large chunks
- 1 red pepper, cut into large chunks

For the marinade

- 2 kaffir lime leaves (if you don't have kaffir lime leaves, use zest of 1 lime)
- 4 tbsp soy sauce
- 1 tbsp coconut oil, melted
- 250 ml coconut milk
- 3 cloves garlic, crushed
- 1 tbsp medium curry powder
- 1 tbsp raw cane caster sugar
- Handful fresh coriander, finely chopped

For the satay sauce

- 125 g peanut butter (smooth or crunchy – whichever you prefer)
- 2 tbsp soy sauce
- 2 tsp brown sugar
- 50 ml warm water
- 2 tbsp lime juice
- 1 clove garlic, crushed
- 2 cm fresh ginger, grated
- 1 red chilli, minced, or 1 tsp dried chilli flakes

To serve

- 1–2 limes, cut into wedges
- A few leaves of fresh coriander

Method

FOR THE MARINADE

Grind the kaffir lime leaves using a pestle and mortar. In a large bowl, mix the kaffir lime powder with the rest of the marinade ingredients.

Add in the kebab vegetables and tofu, and stir, ensuring all the chunks are covered with the marinade. Leave to marinate for 30 minutes to an hour.

FOR THE SATAY SAUCE

Mix together all ingredients.

FOR THE KEBABS

Preheat grill to medium-high. Mindfully and with care, arrange the vegetable chunks in a visually appealing way on the skewers by threading the centre of each chunk onto the skewer prongs and gently pressing it along the skewer. Arrange your kebabs in a cast iron skillet or grill pan. Grill for a few minutes until browned, then rotate the skewers and grill the other side until browned. You can do this with heatproof gloves or tongs.

Warm the satay sauce if you wish, and pour into individual dipping bowls. Place two skewers and one dipping bowl on each plate, and serve with satay sauce, a wedge of lime and fresh coriander.

Celeriac adds richness to this earthy variation on dauphinoise potatoes. Serve as a vegetable accompaniment, or with a green or colourful salad as a meal in its own right.

Makes: 1 gratin dish

Ingredients

- 2 packets silken tofu
- 500 ml plant-based milk
- 2 cloves garlic, crushed
- 2 tsp dried parsley
- 2 tsp Dijon mustard or 1 tsp mustard powder
- 6 potatoes, finely sliced
- 1 celeriac, peeled and finely sliced
- 2 tbsp olive oil or butter
- Salt and pepper

Method

Preheat oven to 180°C.

In a jug, stir together the tofu, milk, garlic, parsley and mustard or mustard powder, adding salt and pepper to taste.

Line a lasagne dish with a layer of potatoes, then a layer of celeriac. Spoon over a few spoonfuls of the liquid.

Continue to add layers of vegetables covered with liquid. Top with a little olive oil or a couple of knobs of butter, and sprinkle on more parsley.

Bake for 1 hour.

Add a few capers and chopped gherkins for tang, extra bite and a bit of green if you like.

CELERIAC AND POTATO GRATIN

SOY OR BEESWAX CANDLE IN A JAR

Burning candles can become a lovely part of your dinnertime ritual. According to the Happiness Research Institute in Copenhagen, Danes burn more candles than any other nation, and also consistently come high up in international happiness ratings.

The paraffin wax in most candles gives off fumes and is now recognized as a form of indoor air pollution. Paraffin wax is derived from petroleum, which is drilled out from the ground and refined. Soy and beeswax candles, on the other hand, are wonderfully natural and have a longer burn time. Soy candles are neutral, while beeswax candles are believed to clean the air by releasing negative ions that bind with impurities.

TO MAKE YOUR OWN CANDLE:

You will need

* Candle-making kit or wax pellets
* Heatproof glass bowl or jug (you won't be able to use this again for cooking)
* Wick measuring 10–15 cm longer than the height of the jar – for a 10-cm jar, you'll need a 25-cm wick
* 1 small flat stone
* A reasonably narrow jar

Instructions

Melt beeswax or soy wax pellets in a heatproof bowl sitting in a pan of simmering water – the water should come to two-thirds of the way up the sides of the bowl. Heat gently until the wax melts.

Meanwhile, tie one end of the wick around a stone and drop to the bottom of the jar. Make sure it is in the centre. This acts as an anchor, so the wick remains straight up the centre of your candle. Wrap the free end of the wick around a cocktail or ice lolly stick and rest the two ends of the stick over the rim of the jar, gently tightening the wick and making sure it is in the centre. You can pinch the wick with a clothes peg if it needs securing. Place the jar on some old newspaper sheets to protect your floor or worktop from wax.

Carefully and with a heat-protective glove, pour in wax to 2 cm from the top of the jar. Leave to set. You will notice as it cools, the wax contracts and a dip or crater may appear around the top of the wick. If this happens, melt a little more wax and top up to 1 cm from the rim. Leave to set and trim the wick to 1 cm. These make lovely presents, presented simply with a string tied in a bow around the middle, and perhaps a personal message tucked underneath. I also keep the melted wax pieces you get at the end and re-melt to make a new candle.

BEGIN A SELF-RESPECT RITUAL

We often ask friends how they are feeling, but how often do we extend this basic courtesy to ourselves? Ask yourself how you are feeling every day. You can do this at the same time every day, or at intervals throughout the day if you wish. Check in with yourself, and ask yourself honestly, "How am I feeling today?" If you're not feeling good, is there anything you can do that would make you feel better? You could allow yourself to close a task and start again tomorrow, or have a bath and an early night, or read a favourite book, or phone an old friend. If you're having a below-par day, take a few moments to acknowledge how you're feeling. Everybody has bad days; sometimes it's best to just accept that and move on, and hope that tomorrow will be better.

KEEP A BEDSIDE GRATITUDE LOG

Every night before going to sleep, note down two or three things you appreciated that day. Remember to include yourself in your log. It could be something specific that you feel you did well, something a friend or loved one did or said or simply the sound of birdsong; or you may simply wish to note your appreciation of a comfortable bed, nutritious food in your tummy and a roof over your head. Note down anything that makes you smile and feel warm, such as making time to support a friend, producing something of beauty, a living thing or a small act of kindness.

YOGA BREAK

CORPSE POSE, SAVASANA

Savasana is a practice of gradually focusing on and relaxing one body area at a time, one muscle at a time, and one thought at a time. When you do this practice at the end of every day, it releases stress from your body and can help prepare you physically and mentally for good quality sleep. Use this pose to promote a profound sense of peace and well-being.

- Lie on your back on your yoga mat, with your feet hip-width or wider gently falling out to the sides. Relax your arms alongside your body, with your palms facing up and your hands open and relaxed.

- Allow your breathing to settle.

- Shift your focus around your body from one area to the next, pausing for a few full breaths in each area. As you focus on each muscle and each body area, gently relax that area, with a sense of contentment and peace. If your mind wanders, gently bring it back to the specific area.

- Take your time and be thankful for the breath.

CHOCOLATE AVOCADO MOUSSE

Avocados? In a dessert? Yes! Full of good fats, avocados are perfect for creamy, mousse-like desserts (or indeed, mousse) and pair really well with chocolate.

Serves: Four

Ingredients

- 2 small ripe avocados
- 80 ml non-dairy milk – soya or almond work well
- 4 tbsp maple syrup
- 1 tbsp almond butter
- 1 tbsp arrowroot
- Pinch salt
- 2 tsp vanilla extract
- 25 g cocoa powder
- 175 g chocolate for melting, such as chocolate chips or baking chocolate

Method

Prepare the avocados as per page 83. Chop the avocado into your food processor, then add all the ingredients except the chocolate. Blitz until smooth.

In a heatproof bowl, melt the chocolate over a pan of water on a medium heat. Once melted, add the chocolate to the mixture and blitz again until well combined.

Transfer the mixture to ramekins or glasses, smooth it over and chill in the freezer until fully set – at least 2 hours.

Before serving, get out of the freezer and leave to soften for 5 minutes or so. Top with chopped hazelnuts and sliced strawberries, or your favourite toppings.

If there's any left over, store, covered, in the freezer.

NOTE: Silken tofu can be used in place of avocados, if you prefer.

NO-WASTE TIP

Keep the leftover oats and use them in overnight oats, porridge or a smoothie, or you could use them in a creamy bath by tying the oats in a piece of muslin cloth and suspending it in your bathwater.

OATY BEDTIME BLISS

This is a simple, humble drink to help your mind and body relax and prepare for a restorative night's sleep.

Serves: One

Ingredients

- ½ tsp dried lavender
- 1 tbsp rolled oats
- Freshly boiled water
- Optional: ½–1 tsp malt extract or honey

Method

Place the dried lavender in a large mug. Place the rolled oats in a tea strainer and place the strainer over the mug (or if you don't like floating lavender buds in your drink, you can place them in the strainer too).

Pour the boiled water over until the oats in the strainer are covered. Gently dip the strainer up and down for 2 minutes.

Remove the strainer from the mug. Stir in malt extract or honey if using.

An essential ingredient for well-being and harmony is quality sleep. Create a restful bedtime routine for yourself, perhaps with candles or aromatherapy oils, or a herbal infusion, relaxing bath, yoga sequence or book. Avoid caffeine and other stimulants, and make your bedroom a screen-free sanctuary. Give yourself the opportunity for a full 8 hours' sleep whenever you can, and enjoy the restorative benefits. Plants need their sleep, and we do too!

CHAPTER SIX:
The Mindful Art of Food Preparation

AS YOU LIVE MORE MINDFULLY,
YOU EAT MORE MINDFULLY.

Lani Muelrath

Taking time over the presentation and preparation of the food you are going to eat as well as food you are making for others is a wonderfully giving thing to do, for you are giving your time and your care. Whether it's presenting vegetables in attractive ways, kneading bread or exercising patience and care by nurturing a sourdough starter, really engaging with the small details of the plants you prepare to eat is a fundamental part of the process of mindful eating and appreciation.

RAW

Eating a diet of mostly raw plant-based food means you're benefiting from that immediate connection to the food in its natural state, and also means you are absorbing the full nutritional value of the plant. Some nutrients are destroyed or reduced in the process of cooking, especially water-soluble ones like vitamin C and B vitamins, which are broken down when boiled. Minerals such as potassium, magnesium, calcium, zinc, iron and phosphorus can also lose more than half their nutrients during certain cooking processes. This is why steaming is better than boiling, as veg retains much more of its nutrition. Freezing vegetables fresh retains their nutritional value. In eating raw fruit and veg, you are also respecting the yoga principle of aparigraha (simplicity); raw food requires no cooking or processing.

COOKED

Cooked foods are also beneficial in your diet, as cooking can increase the bioavailability of certain nutrients and antioxidants, such as lycopene and beta carotene. Light heat or steam breaks down some foods into a more digestible form, and roasting is an excellent way to cook vegetables and nuts.

Tomatoes, peppers, carrots, broccoli, spinach, mushrooms and asparagus all gain nutritional benefits and are easier to digest when cooked. Roasted red peppers and carrots break down their cell walls and release more antioxidant carotenoids, mushrooms make more vitamin C available, and tomatoes give us the antioxidant lycopene. Steam broccoli and spinach, and bake, steam or sauté asparagus.

SOURDOUGH

The slow-rising quality of sourdough breads is favoured by many for being easier to digest and for its superior flavour. Sourdough is bread made without adding yeast – "wild yeast" and lactic acid bacteria present in flour allow it to naturally ferment, if given time, into a wonderful, ripe, living "starter". During the bread-making process, the starter ferments the sugars in the dough, helping the bread rise and acquire its characteristic taste. Lactic acid bacteria are present in other fermented foods such as kimchi, yoghurt, kefir, pickles and sauerkraut.

FOR YOUR STARTER
Ingredients

- 1 kg packet any wholemeal, stoneground flour, such as rye, spelt or wheat
- Water

Method

DAY ONE

Thoroughly clean a large mason jar. Add in 200 g wholemeal flour.

In a clean jug, measure 200 ml tepid water, by adding cold tap water and adding a little boiled water from a kettle. Pour this into the jar and mix. Seal the jar and leave in a warm place for 24 hours.

DAY TWO

Pop open the lid and stir in 100 g more flour and 100 ml more tepid water. The ratio is very simple: however many grams of flour you put in, add in the same number of millilitres of water.

Reseal your jar and return it to its warm place.

DAY THREE

Pop the lid again and you should notice some bubbles and a slight tang beginning to develop. Your starter has begun to ferment! This is a good time to welcome it into your life with a name and a ceremonial bow: we named ours Doughreen.

Repeat the same step as for day two: add in 100 g flour and 100 ml water.

DAY FOUR

Your starter should now be bubbling happily and developing a fermented, fruity aroma. You

DID YOU KNOW?

Researchers believe sourdough's prebiotic composition and probiotic properties (see page 184) are responsible for making it easier to digest than bread fermented with brewer's yeast. Sourdough contains higher levels of antioxidants than other breads, while its lower phytic acid levels allow your body to absorb the nutrients it contains more readily. It is believed that sourdough fermentation may break down gluten better than baker's yeast, so sourdough's lower gluten content may also make it literally easier to stomach for anyone sensitive to gluten.

are now ready to bake bread with your living starter. You can use it in any bread recipe that calls for dried or fresh yeast.

To keep your starter going, continue to feed it every day or every other day (depending on how often you wish to make bread) with 50/100 g flour, and 50/100 ml water. I find it easiest to do this with a coffee measuring spoon – I add in 1 spoon flour and 1 spoon water every few days to keep the starter going. The fruity, fermented smell will continue to deepen over the next few days as your starter matures, provided you keep feeding it.

If you are going away or don't plan to use it for a while, you can freeze it in a tub or refrigerate your jar, feeding it once every four or five days. You can also freeze part of your starter – half, say – for use another time, or to give to a friend, to share your sourdough initiation. To top up your own starter if it's getting low, simply add a little more flour and water than usual – 150–200 g/ml – and it will soon revive. You can keep a starter going indefinitely.

FOR YOUR LOAF

Take 200 g of your starter and mix in a large mixing bowl with 250 ml tepid water. Add 400 g strong white flour and 1½ tsp salt. Mix together into a sloppy dough, using either your fingers or a wooden spoon.

Knead for 8–10 minutes until your dough is supple. Add a little extra flour if it's too sticky, or water if it's too stiff. Pour a little extra virgin olive oil over, place in an oiled bread tin and cover with a damp cloth. Leave in a warm place for 8–12 hours, by which time it should have grown in size.

Bake on the floor of your oven at 230°C for 30–40 minutes. Check it at 30 minutes. A golden crust will have formed. To check if it's ready, remove the loaf from the tin with oven gloves and tap the base with your fingernail. If it's ready, it should make a hollow sound. If it makes a doughy thud, return it to the oven for another 5–10 minutes. Remove from oven and leave to cool on a rack. Slice, serve and enjoy!

TROUBLESHOOTING

If nothing seems to be happening after three or four days, make sure the place where your jar is sitting is warm enough and give it another few days. A temperature of around 25–29°C is ideal, but this may not be possible in your home; aim to have it at 22°C or above if possible. If it is still lifeless, start again with a new batch of flour. Make sure the water is tepid when you add it (around 30°C is ideal) and the place you are storing it is warm. If any mould grows (this is uncommon), discard immediately.

Make sure you very carefully open the lid of your jar daily to release the pressure that has built up. When it is really active, you may need to do this two or three times a day. Some people prefer to keep theirs in a plastic box for this reason.

This is only a brief introduction; whole books are written on sourdough fermentation and baking. Enjoy experimenting with your ripening starter.

TURKISH FLATBREAD
WITH NIGELLA AND SESAME SEEDS

Enjoy these beautiful soft flatbreads, with a delicate cumin-like flavour from the nigella seeds.

Makes: 6 flatbreads

Ingredients

- 400 g strong flour (your choice of white or wholemeal, or half and half)
- 1 packet dried yeast, or 1 tbsp fresh yeast
- 1½ tsp sea salt
- 2 tbsp yoghurt (natural yoghurt or vegan alternative)
- 2 tbsp extra virgin olive oil, plus extra for oiling
- 260 ml lukewarm water

For the glaze

- 1 tbsp yoghurt
- 1–2 tsp each of nigella and sesame seeds

Method

Place the flour, yeast, salt, yoghurt, oil and water in a mixing bowl. Mix with your hands, adding a little more water if needed, until you have a soft but firm dough. Knead in the bowl until it has become supple and stretchy. This is one of life's great mindful activities: touching the ingredients and combining them with your hands before baking them – observe the different sensations as you mix dry, wet, cold, warm, oily and sticky, see how the consistency changes, and notice that connection with the food. Pour a little oil over and rotate your dough ball until it is coated in oil. Cover and leave to rise for 1 hour.

Preheat oven to 220°C. Divide the dough into six even pieces. Shape each into a ball and roll gently into circles, ovals or uneven shapes.

Using the blunt side of a dinner knife, draw a criss-cross pattern on the top, with lines 4 cm apart.

With an egg brush, brush a little yoghurt on top for a glaze, then sprinkle with nigella and sesame seeds. Bake for 10 minutes.

VARIATIONS

You could use spelt or khorasan flour – ancient heritage grains – instead of the flour, or add 2–3 tbsp sourdough starter to give the bread a slightly different character.

SERVING SUGGESTION

This bread works well with Turkish or Greek dishes, including imam bayildi (see page 122), butter bean dip (see page 68), Greek salads or any roasted veg dish.

It can also be used as a naan bread substitute to accompany curries – nigella seeds have a cumin-type flavour.

It is also delicious simply served as a snack or starter, with a small bowl each of extra virgin olive oil and balsamic vinegar for dipping. Just tear off pieces of bread and dip.

This traditional bread is dense and delicious for a pick-me-up at any time of day, and goes with anything, savoury or sweet. This version uses jumbo oats instead of wheat flour.

Makes: 1 loaf

Ingredients

- 400 ml natural yoghurt (traditionally buttermilk is used)
- 1 tbsp treacle
- 250 g jumbo oats
- 1 heaped tsp baking soda
- ½ tsp sea salt

Method

Preheat oven to 200°C.

Place the yoghurt and treacle in a bowl and stir well.

Add in the oats, baking soda and salt and mix together to form a loose dough. Don't worry about the consistency; the oats will absorb moisture during baking.

Pour into a greased loaf tin or circular tin, sprinkle with oats and bake for 35 minutes. If you are using a circular tin, you can mark a cross on top with a blunt knife before baking.

VARIATIONS

You could add in 2 tbsp seeds (sunflower seeds, or a seed mix) into the mix, and sprinkle a few on top. For a sweeter bread add some chopped apricots and figs, or try 2 tbsp chopped sundried tomatoes and basil for a savoury version.

SODA
BREAD

NO-KNEAD CIABATTA

If you place a bowl of water in the back of the oven, the steam it gives off will give your bread a crunchier crust.

Beautiful, crusty ciabatta with no need to knead? Really? Yes, really, except you'll have to wait. The trick is to mix the ingredients together the day before you wish to eat it, as the dough requires 18 hours to rise.

Makes: 2 ciabattas (or "2 ciabatte" if you want to be authentic)

Ingredients

- 500 g strong flour (your choice)
- ¼ tsp dried yeast
- 1½ tsp sea salt
- 470 ml lukewarm water

Method

Mix ingredients together in a mixing bowl and cover. Leave in a warm place for 18 hours.

Preheat oven to 200°C. Take your dough and place on a floured surface. Flatten slightly and fold the sides in to the centre. Gently pull the dough into two pieces and form into loose rectangular shapes – ciabatta literally translates from Italian as "slipper".

Bake on a tray on the floor of the oven for 30–35 minutes.

Why not chop a few olives and poke them into one of the doughs before baking? You can eat or share one of your ciabattas and freeze the other for another day.
I also like to add 3 tbsp sourdough starter and 2 tbsp extra virgin olive oil, and use 60 ml less water,
for flavour and digestive reasons.

Healthy traditional Scottish oatcakes provide the perfect lunchtime snack to accompany salads, soups and dips.

Makes: 16–20

Ingredients

- 250 g fine oatmeal
- 60 g/ml fat (almond butter, butter or olive oil)
- 2 pinches sea salt
- Cold water as required

Method

Preheat oven to 180°C.

Mix ingredients, adding a little water to make a soft but not sticky dough. Roll directly onto a baking tray liner and cut with a round cutter (or any shape you prefer). Re-roll and repeat with the offcuts. Press down on each firmly with your hand or the base of a glass to avoid crumbly oatcakes.

Bake at 180°C for around 20 minutes, until they are turning golden.

These keep well in an airtight container. Milled seeds are a good substitute for part of the oatmeal, if desired.

VARIATION

1 tsp ground dried lavender added to the mix gives these a stunning flavour.

RUSTIC
OATCAKES

VEGETABLE FLOWERS

Taking time over presentation is worth every second, for you get to enjoy the process and the beauty of the finished product. Vegetables can easily be cut into sticks of any thickness for dipping, but a more interesting presentation that always goes down well is vegetable flowers. Cucumber, tomato and radishes work well.

Hold your washed vegetable against a chopping board with your non-dominant hand and hold a sharp knife in your cutting hand. The vegetable should be placed on its side with the top to the left and the bottom to the right.

Draw an imaginary zigzag line around your vegetable or fruit. For a tomato, this imaginary zigzag will be horizontally across the centre of the fruit. Press the point of the knife into the tomato to make the first cut, cutting a diagonal line around 2 cm long and 3 cm deep, from top right to bottom left.

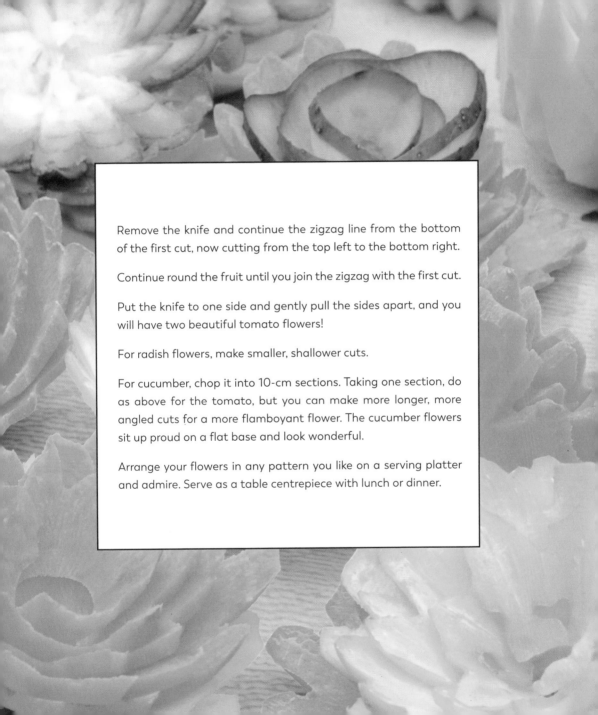

Remove the knife and continue the zigzag line from the bottom of the first cut, now cutting from the top left to the bottom right.

Continue round the fruit until you join the zigzag with the first cut.

Put the knife to one side and gently pull the sides apart, and you will have two beautiful tomato flowers!

For radish flowers, make smaller, shallower cuts.

For cucumber, chop it into 10-cm sections. Taking one section, do as above for the tomato, but you can make more longer, more angled cuts for a more flamboyant flower. The cucumber flowers sit up proud on a flat base and look wonderful.

Arrange your flowers in any pattern you like on a serving platter and admire. Serve as a table centrepiece with lunch or dinner.

KIMCHI

Kimchi never goes off; it ripens. But the riper it is, the sourer it becomes, so it's entirely up to your taste buds if it's still edible! It can be used in all manner of dishes to give them a kick. Stir a few tablespoons into stews or soups, or spread onto bread or crackers.

Fermented food is good for gut health and is an eco-thrifty way to use up leftover vegetables. Kimchi is a combination of fermented vege-tables and salt. It's rich in probiotics and vitamins A, B and C, and is a staple served in many South Korean households.

Ingredients

- 1 medium napa cabbage (also known as Chinese cabbage), chopped into 1-cm cubes
- 1 tbsp table salt
- Water
- 1 carrot, grated
- 1 tbsp caster sugar

- 1 tbsp chilli flakes
- 1 garlic clove, minced
- 1 thumbnail-sized piece fresh root ginger, minced
- 4 spring onions, sliced
- 5 radishes, sliced

Method

Place the cabbage in a bowl with the salt, cover with water, then pop a plate on top of the cabbage so that it's submerged in the salted water and leave for six hours.

Drain the cabbage but keep the liquid to one side.

Mix the rest of the ingredients in a bowl and add the cabbage.

Decant into a jar, squashing the mixture down so that it's compacted. Pour over the salted water so that it covers the cabbage. Screw on the lid securely.

Leave for five days to ferment, but make sure you remember to open the jar once a day to allow the gas to escape!

Other fermented foods you could try introducing into your diet are kombucha and miso. Kombucha is an infusion made by fermenting sweetened green or black tea using a culture of bacteria and yeast, known as the "mother" or "mushroom". Miso is a Japanese seasoning made by fermenting soybeans with salt and the fungus kōji. The resulting paste is used in sauces, pickles and spreads, and used as the base for misoshiru, a miso soup. Rich in vitamins and minerals and high in protein, miso is widely used in Japanese cooking. Variations include the addition of rice, barley or seaweed. Miso is typically salty but some versions can be sweet, fruity or savoury, depending on the specific ingredients and fermentation process used.

CHUTNEYS

Chutneys are an excellent and delicious way to breathe new life into old fruit and veg, and add flavour and interest to a sandwich, wrap or curry. Chutney is a combination of just about any fruit or veg you like, flavoured with spices and cooked with vinegar and sugar to a thick, dark, jam-like consistency. The cooking smells are marvellous.

Soft, overripe vegetables are ideal. For a chunky chutney, dice your fruit or veg into chunks. For a more spreadable chutney, finely chop the vegetables. Use stainless steel or enamel pans. Using leftover veg in this way is the ultimate way to honour the plant and the planet and waste nothing. If you make too much, give away jars you won't use as gifts with pretty cloth lids.

Makes: 6–8 jars each

TOMATO, RED PEPPER AND CHILLI CHUTNEY

Ingredients

- 500 g tomatoes, cored and chopped into chunks
- 2 red peppers, sliced into 3-cm strips
- 2 onions, halved and sliced
- 1–2 red chillies, finely chopped
- 750 ml white wine vinegar
- 150 g raw cane caster sugar, brown sugar or molasses
- 1 tsp paprika
- 1 tsp sea salt

Method

Place the tomatoes, red peppers, onions, chilli, vinegar and sugar in a large saucepan. Bring to the boil then reduce the heat to low, maintaining a rolling simmer. Cook for 90 minutes, until soft and thick, stirring occasionally.

Stir in the paprika and salt. Pour into clean jars and leave to cool before sealing.

FIG CHUTNEY

As above, but use 700 g fresh figs in place of the tomatoes and peppers, omit the chillies and paprika and use brown sugar instead of caster sugar.

PEACH AND APRICOT CHUTNEY

As above, but use 500 g peaches instead of tomatoes, and 200 g fresh or dried apricots instead of peppers. Omit the chillies and paprika and use brown sugar instead of caster sugar.

Serves: Four

Ingredients

- 400 g tipo 00 flour
- 240 ml lukewarm water
- 2 tbsp olive oil
- 1 tsp salt

Method

Place your flour, water, olive oil and salt in a large mixing bowl. Mix together with your fingers.

Knead for 8–10 minutes, cover with a damp tea towel and leave to rest for half an hour. When you return, the dough should feel soft and silky – 00 is a very fine milling size of flour.

On a floured surface, roll out with a rolling pin until it is 2 mm thick, then cut into long strips. Or if you have a pasta maker, feed your pasta through the roller, turning the handle, taking care to support the hanging end of the dough. This can be a little fiddly – take your time. If there is a spare pair of hands in the house, you can call on them to help support the dough as you feed it through the maker. You can re-feed your sheet of dough through the pasta maker, setting it to a narrower width each time. Then re-feed your dough sheet into the machine. You can choose from a selection of settings, from thin spaghetti to wide tagliatelle.

Hang over the backs of your kitchen chairs to dry. Take care to make sure each strand is separated from the next, otherwise they can clump together.

When you're ready to cook your fresh pasta, boil it for 1–2 minutes. Anything more and it may turn into a sticky mess.

MINDFUL REMINDER

As you knead and feed the dough through the pasta maker, notice its changing consistency and think about how this came from ears of wheat.

MAKING YOUR OWN PASTA

PASTA PRIMAVERA

A fresh, light pasta dish full of vibrant spring greens. This is particularly great in May, when asparagus is in season, and if you opt to make your own pasta, you can enjoy a soothing and satisfying mindful experience.

Serves: Four

Ingredients

- 400 g fresh tagliatelle
- 3 tbsp extra virgin olive oil
- 1 clove garlic, crushed
- 150 g fresh young asparagus, blanched, cut into bite-sized pieces
- 150 g fresh or frozen peas
- 100 g young spinach
- Zest and juice of 1 lemon
- Large handful fresh herbs, such as mint, basil, dill and parsley, chopped
- Salt and pepper
- Handful toasted pine nuts and olive oil to serve

Method

Cook the tagliatelle for 4 minutes in boiling water, so it still has a bite. Drain.

Meanwhile, fry the garlic for 2 minutes in the oil, over a medium heat. Add the asparagus, peas and spinach and fry for a further 1–2 minutes then remove from heat – the most common mistake is overcooking. Stir in the pasta, the lemon zest and juice and half the herbs, and season.

Divide between four pasta bowls, and garnish with toasted pine nuts, a drizzle of extra virgin olive oil and the rest of the fresh herbs.

CHAPTER SEVEN:
An Ayurveda Garden

❖ ❖ ❖ ❖ ❖

TO NURTURE A GARDEN IS TO FEED
NOT JUST THE BODY, BUT THE SOUL.

Alfred Austin

In Ayurveda, everything is connected. Food comes from the earth, and ultimately returns to the earth and becomes earth, in the life cycle of decomposition and regeneration.

Thousands of years before modern medicine, the sages of India developed this holistic science that recognizes at its heart the mind-body connection (ayur means life, and veda means science or knowledge). Ayurveda survives today as a mind-body health system and ethos that focuses on exercise, yoga and meditation as well as diet and connection with the land. The concept of balance is also central to Ayurvedic thinking, encompassing a balanced diet as well as mental and spiritual balance and well-being. It also extends to reflect the symbiosis of humans as existing within nature, and the balance of our inner nature with the environment (external nature).

One element of this balanced dietary philosophy is to eat a rainbow – a range of differently coloured foods. This makes food selection, preparation and propagation a source of sensory wonder and joy.

GROWING YOUR OWN

Growing your own is an intrinsic part of deepening your connection with food and makes sense on so many levels. It's economical and convenient and means you can be 100 per cent assured that your produce is organic. It also reduces your carbon footprint in terms of food miles and natural food production compared with large-scale intensive growing. And how satisfying to know the total distance from farm to fork is only a few metres instead of halfway across the world! The physical benefits of gardening are also manifold: labouring in the garden is physical exercise, you are soaking up vitamin D

and the exertion releases endorphins, which alleviate stress and lower blood pressure. More than anything, however, it increases your understanding of the natural life processes of growing plants, and the enormous satisfaction of observing something grow from a tiny seed into a fruiting, leafing source of food.

If you live in an apartment with no outside space, a window box or pots on the windowsill can be enough to grow a range of fresh fruit, vegetables and herbs, and if you plan it carefully you could have a continuous supply all season, while shaving a fair amount off your grocery bill. Allotments and community gardening initiatives are another way to grow your own, if you don't have the means to do so at home – search for schemes near you. Salad leaves and herbs can also be grown in the kitchen, ensuring fresh leaves all year round.

You can compost any peels and uncooked plant waste in a small caddy placed outdoors in the sun, then use the nutrient-rich compost to grow more plant food!

Replacing one-fifth of the food you eat with home-grown produce could reduce your annual carbon footprint by nearly 32 kg of CO_2.

HERB JARS

These jars provide an attractive and convenient way of growing your own herbs on a windowsill for daily use. You can also grow chillies in this way.

You will need

- Seeds to grow herb plants, such as basil, mint, parsley, thyme, oregano, chives, dill, lemon balm, rosemary and coriander
- A selection of jam jars – pick shapes you find appealing
- Gravel, grit or small stones
- Organic multi-purpose or potting compost
- Water

Instructions

Clean your jam jars with washing-up liquid and warm water, rinse and leave to dry.

Fill the base of your jars with gravel, grit or stones – make sure it's at least 5 cm in depth. This layer is vital for drainage, to prevent mould from rotting your plant roots.

Fill the jars about two-thirds full with compost. Plant three herb seeds in each jar.

Once shoots start to form, add more compost around the base of each plant. Water your plants and place them on a windowsill. Choose a shadier spot if your choice of herb prefers shade.

Trim your plants regularly to avoid them getting stringy and bolting.

Now you're all set to enjoy the taste, sight and smell of herbs all year round, and they've travelled zero food miles!

TOILET-ROLL TUBE PLUGS

Empty, unbleached toilet-roll tubes make ideal containers for growing crops from seed and mean an end to plastic pots.

Fold in one end of the toilet roll to form a small pot. Fill the container two-thirds of the way up with compost. Place a seed in each container (or follow packet instructions – sometimes two seeds are recommended per hole), then cover the seeds with a little more compost and moisten with water. Find a suitable flat-based waterproof tray to house your toilet-roll planters so that the water doesn't soak through onto your windowsill or floor. A sunny spot will help the seedlings to sprout.

Once the seedlings are well established, if you have space in a garden, you can plant the whole plant – including the container – into the ground or in larger pots. The cardboard will protect the roots from pests before it biodegrades. Keep your seedlings moist and within as little as four weeks you could have your first crop of rocket and lettuce leaves. Pinch off the outer leaves, wash them, and you have ready-made salad!

PLANTS TO GROW IN YOUR TOILET-ROLL POTS:

- Lettuce
- Rocket
- Radish
- Spring onion
- Parsley
- Cherry tomatoes
- Dill
- Sage
- Aloe vera (the edible variety)
- Chillies
- Peas
- Broad beans
- Spinach

You can also start your seedlings off in a used unbleached teabag. Simply break open the teabag and place a seedling inside – the nitrogen in the tea promotes growth. Then pop the teabag and seedling into compost.

PLOTTING YOUR GARDEN

Note down things that you'd like to grow in a journal or on a piece of paper. Then, all you need to do is buy the seeds from a garden centre or online and you're all set to have your very own micro-scale smallholding!

Growing a wildflower patch in any size of garden is wonderful, to attract bees, butterflies, moths and wasps, which pollinate the plants that we eat – and to simply enjoy observing the natural beauty of the plants as they grow and flower. If you don't have a garden, you can grow wildflowers in a pot or window box. Choose a mix native to your area from a seed specialist, and you will be helping to preserve the biodiversity of your particular area.

BE ROOTED,

BE JOYFUL,

BE FREE

CRANACHAN

This Scottish dessert is a delightful surprise combination of foraged fresh raspberries, oatmeal and cream, with optional honeyed whisky.

Serves: Two

Ingredients

- 80 g medium oatmeal
- 2 tbsp agave nectar (or honey is traditionally used, for non-vegans)
- 250 g/ml whipped cream substitute such as cashew cream or soy cream (or whipped cream is traditional), chilled
- 200 g raspberries – foraged, home-grown or shop-bought
- Optional: 2–4 tsp whisky
- Optional: rolled oats or seeds

Method

To toast the oatmeal, arrange it on a baking tray and grill under a medium grill for a few minutes until you notice the warm, toasting smell. Alternatively, you can fry the oatmeal for 2–3 minutes in a dry frying pan.

Fold the oatmeal and agave nectar into the whipped cream. If using whisky, fold it in at this stage.

Place a few raspberries in the bottom of two wine glasses, tumblers or glass dessert bowls. Spoon half of the oatmeal and cream mixture into the glasses, forming a clear layer.

Arrange a second layer of raspberries and a second layer of oatmeal cream in each glass. Top with raspberries and an optional sprinkling of rolled oats or seeds.

SENSORY FORAGE

A walk in any wild, natural setting can be transformed into a wonderfully mindful activity if you approach it with curiosity and appreciation. Wild environments are naturally stimulating, and pausing to observe with all your senses can really help you to reconnect with the wilderness. Add in foraging for wild foods, and you can take a mindful walk to a whole new level of wonder and purpose.

Stick to well-known plants you feel confident identifying, such as wild garlic, blackberries, raspberries and elderflowers, and avoid anything that may have been sprayed or that is too close to the road.

◆ Bring a water bottle of fresh water in your backpack – not only for drinking, but for rinsing any edibles you forage.

◆ Walk tall and feel your feet rooted through the ground with each step. Swing your arms and feel your heart beating and your breath deepening as you walk. Be mindful of sensations, smells, sounds and sights around you.

◆ Look up, and observe the world above you – the canopy of trees, the sky and clouds, the wildlife. Allow yourself to absorb the wonders of nature through all your senses.

◆ Now look down, and observe the living world at your feet. Kneel, sit or squat on the ground and take time to notice all the tiny details you've never noticed before. It can be quite magical and humbling to notice something new.

- Observe the plant you are foraging. For instance, if it is a blackberry bush, observe the shape and feel of the leaves. Notice their smell. Focus in on the thorns, and admire the plant for this clever defence mechanism, to protect against predators that would otherwise attack the plant. Touch a berry. Feel how it is attached to the plant. Gently pull it away. Taking your time, observe, smell and taste it. Notice the flavour and texture. Be grateful to the plant for this gift.

- If it is wild garlic you are picking, observe the vivid green and feel the smoothness of the leaves. Notice the strong smell of the leaves, especially when you fold, tear or crush them. Tear off a piece, and observe the leaf structure and the liquid inside. Wash with a little water, then chew a piece slowly and marvel as the flavour explodes in your mouth.

- Whatever the item, take time and care to really notice it and its particular characteristics. Be thankful for these offerings from nature.

 If you wish to extend your foraging skills, book yourself onto a foraging course with an expert. Never pick anything you haven't identified as 100 per cent safe to eat – many plants as well as fungi and berries are highly toxic, and fatal if consumed.

FORAGED WILD GARLIC PESTO

The first crop of chives will be ready just as wild garlic is really coming into its own in spring. Combine the two for a really fresh-tasting – and frankly quite powerful – homemade pesto. Thoroughly wash the wild garlic after you pick it and ensure it is dry before storing it in the fridge ahead of making this recipe.

Makes: 1 jar

Ingredients

- 1 large bunch wild garlic
- 150 g chives
- 50 g pine nuts
- 150 ml olive oil
- 60 g Parmesan
- Salt and black pepper
- 1 tbsp lemon juice

Method

Blitz the garlic, chives, pine nuts and olive oil in a blender until well combined but still a little rough. Add more oil if you'd like the consistency to be smoother.

Add the cheese, salt and pepper to taste. Stir in the lemon juice just before serving, or at the end if making to store.

HOW TO SPROUT LENTILS

Ancient civilizations have been sprouting grains and pulses for millennia. Sprouted foods are also known as macrobiotic foods. When you sprout lentils, you are beginning the plant's natural germination process, which changes the composition of the lentils. Sprouting augments the bioavailability of nutrients by neutralizing the phytic acid in lentils – effectively this means more vitamins, minerals and fibre can be absorbed by your body as they're digested. When soaked in water, the lentil "wakes up" and begins to sprout, whereas unsprouted grains are dormant, with more of their nutrients locked up. Enzymes work their magic by breaking down growth inhibitors, making nutrients easier to absorb, especially B vitamins and carotene. Sprouting also helps to break down some of the naturally occurring sugars in lentils that can contribute to stomach gas.

You can also sprout other beans, pulses and grains in this way. This is an excellent mindful and healthful gardening option if you don't have a garden or balcony.

- Place your desired quantity of dried lentils in a clean jar and cover with water. Cover the jar with a clean muslin cloth and secure with a rubber band around the rim – choose a fine cloth with a loose weave. Leave overnight in a cool, clean spot.

- Drain the water, rinse the lentils (they will have tripled in size) and replace the cloth lid (make sure you wash your hands first).

If you would like to bring more macrobiotic foods into your diet, you can also buy sprouted flours and sprouted breads, in which the grain has been sprouted then dried and ground.

- Turn the jar upside down on a clean surface and sit it on top of two chopsticks laid under the rim like railway lines, for air circulation and drainage. Leave overnight.

- Rinse and drain again. Sprouted lentils will grow white tails (shoots) and are ready to eat after two days – they don't need to be cooked, but to be on the safe side, you can boil your sprouted lentils vigorously for 2 minutes before consuming/preparing. Boiling kills bacteria including E. coli.

- Once sprouted, refrigerate and eat the same day, within 12 hours. You can eat them raw or cooked. Use them in salads, in breads, on their own as a snack or in any recipe that calls for dried or cooked lentils (you can make sprouted lentil soup for example).

WARNING!

Several cases of food poisoning have been attributed to sprouted grains, beans and pulses. Make sure you wash and drain your lentils thoroughly every 24 hours and be sure to allow ventilation. Discard immediately into the rubbish – not the compost – if there is any smell or sign of mould. Sterilizing your jar first and keeping it in a cool, clean place while sprouting will help to prevent contamination.

GUT FEELING

The human body contains trillions of microbes, most of which are beneficial. Our biggest microbe population lives in our gut, where these tiny bacteria are busy playing a critical role in digestion, immune function and weight regulation. Keep them happy and healthy with a balanced, nutritious diet.

TIPS FOR A HEALTHY GUT

- Eat a wide range of plant-based foods. Different foods feed different microbes – just like you, they have their own micro food preferences!

- Eat plenty of fibre. Fresh vegetables, fruit, pulses, nuts and wholegrains are ideal.

- Avoid highly processed foods.

DID YOU KNOW?

We have an estimated 500 million neurons in our gut, hence why it is sometimes referred to as our "second brain" – so the notion of our "gut feeling" is in fact backed up by biology. Microbes have been around for 3.5 billion years, and less than one in 20 causes disease.

PRE V. PRO?

Prebiotics – complex carbohydrates such as vegetables and whole grains – "fertilize" our gut bacteria and promote the development of a diverse community of "friendly" microbes. They are non-digestible fibres that feed the beneficial bacteria in our gut. How lovely to know your body is host to this happy internal village!

Probiotics, such as fermented foods, some cheeses and live yoghurt – yoghurt fermented with live culture bacteria such as *Lactobacillus acidophilus* – are foods that contain live bacteria thought to be beneficial to gut health.

POTATOES IN A BUCKET

Potatoes are very easy to grow in a bucket. Simply leave an organic potato in a dry, dark cupboard and it will soon sprout. Once you can see shoots forming, place the potato in a large bucket outdoors lined with stones or bricks at the bottom for drainage, then fill with compost. Disease-resistant seed potatoes are sold for this purpose, but I've always grown a reasonable crop from sprouted organic potatoes. Potatoes can rot in waterlogged conditions, so drill a few holes around the base of the bucket. You can arrange up to nine sprouted potatoes around the bucket, depending on its size. Cover with a further 15 cm compost. Allow the rain to water them naturally, or water during dry spells. After 90–120 days, once they have flowered and the flowers have wilted, simply empty the bucket onto a sheet of tarpaulin, plastic or hessian, and have fun picking out all the potatoes, noticing the feel and earthy smell of the soil on your hands. You should have 5–10 new potatoes for each one you planted. Marvel at the ease of growing this wonderful crop! Tip the compost back into the bucket for reuse. Wash the potatoes, dry and store in a hessian sack or a cool, dark box or cupboard.

A small open jar of dried peas placed on a shelf in the cupboard with the sprouting potatoes will absorb any moisture and stop the tubers rotting. The same goes for the harvested potatoes.

GROW AN ONION
FROM AN ONION

With care and water, you can grow a new onion from an old onion in 90–120 days! This kind of growing is wonderfully rewarding, demonstrating the continuous potential of plants to regenerate. If you can keep this going year-round you could have a perpetual supply of onions!

- Place your onion on a chopping board and, using a sharp knife, cut off the bottom and remove the outer peel. Your onion section should be about 2.5 cm from root base to cut.
- Leave your onion section to dry for 24 hours and, of course, use the remainder in any suitable recipe.
- Fill a small jar or bottle with water and rest your onion section on the rim, with the cut-side up and the base submerged in the water. If you don't have any narrow-necked jars, you can poke four cocktail sticks into the flesh of the onion near the cut, and suspend the onion into the jar, with the sticks resting over the rim.
- After two to three days, you will notice white shoots appearing. It is now ready to plant in soil. The centre layers will rise and sprout and the onion will regenerate a new onion.

DID YOU KNOW?

Onions are nutrient-dense – high in vitamins, minerals and fibre and low in calories. They are a particularly trusty source of vitamins C, B and potassium, as well as allicin. According to various studies, their potent anti-inflammatory properties contained in the flavonoid antioxidant quercetin may lower your risk of heart disease and certain cancers. Another study showed a reduction in cholesterol levels after consumption of raw red onions.

SPROUTING GARLIC

Garlic can be wonderfully self-perpetuating: if you separate a bulb of garlic into individual cloves and plant the cloves a few centimetres apart, each clove will grow a new bulb of garlic. One bulb of garlic can therefore regenerate ten to 14 new bulbs, so you theoretically never need to buy another bulb again if you continue to plant one or two cloves and eat the rest! Store in a cool, dry cupboard over winter – in France, they sell them as hanging edible decorations in pretty plaits. Yours will be smaller than these in all likelihood, but the flavour and nutrition will be concentrated and they'll taste all the better for having been home-grown.

Garlic is antiviral, antibacterial, antifungal and immune-boosting, and has been shown to reduce the incidence of colds by 63 per cent compared with a placebo, and reduce the length of symptoms by 70 per cent (US National Center for Biotechnology Information). Allicin in garlic also offers reported cancer-combatting benefits. According to various studies, it encourages the production of glutathione S-transferase, an enzyme which helps to kill cancer cells, eliminate toxins and protect healthy cells from free radicals which can cause cells to mutate and become malignant. Consuming garlic also offers protection to our heart and blood vessels by lowering our blood level of homocysteine, an amino acid linked to cardiovascular disease. It really is a superfood!

ELDERBERRY, BLACKBERRY AND RASPBERRY CRUMBLE

This beautiful hearty crumble is a wonderful warmer once autumn has arrived. Forage for wild elderberries, blackberries and raspberries and eat in season, or freeze for a taste of autumn at any time of year. This crumble uses oats instead of flour, and extra virgin rapeseed oil instead of butter. Simple and delicious. *Serves: Four*

Ingredients

For the filling

- 100 g elderberries, fresh or frozen
- 200 g blackberries, fresh or frozen
- 200 g raspberries, fresh or frozen
- 60 g soft brown sugar
- Optional: 50 g flaked almonds, pre-roasted for 5 minutes if you like

For the crumble topping

- 250 g rolled oats (porridge oats, not jumbo oats)
- 100 g flaxseeds, flaxseed mix or ground almonds
- 100 ml rapeseed oil
- 60 g raw cane caster sugar
- Optional: small pinch cinnamon or mixed spice

> ## WARNING!
>
> Elderberries can only be consumed cooked. They cannot be eaten raw as the seeds contain cyanide-inducing glycosides. Cooking them breaks down these compounds. They are an excellent seasonal source of vitamin C and have cold-combatting powers – in tests, black elder has been shown to shorten the duration of colds and flu by inhibiting the viruses' ability to penetrate cells. Elderberries (and blackberries) are a good source of anthocyanin antioxidants. If you don't have an elder tree nearby, you can substitute extra blackberries.

Method

Preheat oven to 180°C. Arrange elderberries, blackberries and raspberries in the base of a pie or lasagne dish. Frozen berries work just as well as fresh berries – you don't need to defrost them first. Sprinkle sugar and flaked almonds over.

Place the crumble topping ingredients together in a bowl. Mix with fingertips into a breadcrumb-like consistency. Sprinkle this evenly over the crumble filling.

Bake for 35–40 minutes, until golden and bubbling.

Serve with your choice of cream and enjoy the bite of the berries and the textures of the flaked almonds and topping ingredients, combined with the rich, soul-feeding flavours.

VARIATIONS

Rhubarb is a wonderful crumble option in late spring. Use 500 g rhubarb in place of the berries.

Apple and raspberry also works well. Use 300 g apples and 200 g raspberries (fresh or frozen).

FRESH FOOD
PREPARED WITH
LOVE IS THE
GREATEST GIFT

MY PERSONAL MINDFUL KITCHEN JOURNEY

If you've been keeping a food journal, jot down words, phrases or visuals that will help you to prepare, cook, eat, grow, reflect upon and develop a deeper connection with plant foods. Which elements would you like to focus on? Note down any words that will inspire you.

CONCLUSION

I hope you have enjoyed reading about how to develop a deeper connection with the food that you eat and a clearer understanding of the mind-body link when it comes to diet. Even if it is just one small step at a time, I hope you are able to incorporate some elements into your daily schedule, in a way that feels right for you. Even if one small aspect works for you, that is enough.

Remember, our relationship with food is lifelong, so this journey is a long-term one. Don't worry if you don't feel like serenity itself, bottled and corked; the important thing is that you are inspired to value natural, nourishing foods, and appreciate the wonderful vigour they can give to your life. Healthy food deserves our respect, as much as we too deserve our own respect, as humans each on our own little journey through this life.

I wish you joy, health, discovery and peace, for in connecting with food, we are connecting with earth and life; we are becoming more grounded; we are demonstrating compassion for the miraculous cycle of life. Like the plants we eat, we are allowing ourselves to become rooted.

Enjoy your very own mindful, plant-based kitchen. Om shanti.

If you're interested in finding out more about our books,
find us on Facebook at **Summersdale Publishers**
and follow us on Twitter at **@Summersdale**.

www.summersdale.com

IMAGE CREDITS